PRAISE FOR *SUPERNATURAL POWER FOR EVERYDAY PEOPLE*

"A book on supernatural living is something one expects from a charismatic or Pentecostal preacher, not a Gospel Coalition blogger. But this is what makes Jared C. Wilson's effort to convey the other-worldly power of the Holy Spirit so intriguing, so infectious. Make no mistake, our God is a supernatural being who works supernaturally."

—KYLE IDLEMAN, author of *not a fan* and *Grace is Greater*

"In his book *Supernatural Power for Everyday People*, Jared C. Wilson points out that the Holy Spirit is not just someone who simply counsels and comforts, but rather our God who convicts and guides. He is the one with the supernatural power to affect our heart, strengthen our resolve, and lead us to action. Whether associated with the holy rollers or one of the frozen chosen—or neither—we all need to embrace this book."

—MIKE COSPER, author of *Recapturing the Wonder*

"Words like *supernatural power* and *Holy Spirit*, in our current cultural and religious moment, have been wielded and to some extent hijacked by pastors with big personalities and big money. Jared brings them back here—and brings us back here—to a simple, biblical, no-fluff look at the 'supernatural power' that changes ordinary, dirt-under-the-fingernails people like you and me. Jared's writing is fluid and thoughtful, efficient and deep, and his theological voice on this subject is so refreshing. As I read *Supernatural Power for Everyday People*, I found myself worshiping as I read, not simply understanding. I found myself craving the Spirit more than His miracles, which is Jared's intention, and it was enlightening for a very normal, hollow soul. Get it. No gimmicks, snakes, or gold dust here—just a real Jesus and a real gospel. Just real power for real people."

author, and worship leader

"Many of us wo   ernaturally work in
our lives, but w   iessages we hear in
various Christia   well to convey how
God supernatural,   , _ we merely submit to his will."

—CALEB KALTENBACH, author of *Messy Grace*

"The word *supernatural* is often mistaken and misused in Christian circles. But in *Supernatural Power for Everyday People*, Wilson corrects the misnomers and rights the mistakes by revealing the supernatural being God reveals himself to be. The Bible is full of supernatural events and experiences that we should embrace and enjoy. Let's live it."

—GREG GILBERT, author of *What is the Gospel?* and *FAVOR*

"With his usual penetrating clarity, Jared C. Wilson describes the delusion of the dull-hearted faith, critiques the shallowness of the consumer-culture faith, and prescribes a pathway to a powerful faith with fresh reflections on everyday practices that awaken us to the Spirit's work in our lives. This book will stir your desire to pursue your faith, guide you to nurture your faith, and encourage you to venture with faith into your everyday relationships."

—GEOFF FOLLAND, leader at Power to Change, Australia

"There is just no way Jared C. Wilson—or anybody else—can speak with so much truth and grace as in these pages except by the power of the Holy Spirit. I found myself confronted and comforted time and time again while reading and desiring to live life more supernaturally and less dependent on my little strength and empty knowledge. I can't wait to share the life-giving truths of this book with my church."

—JAIRO NAMNÚN, executive director of The Gospel Coalition, Spanish

"Tired of slogging through your spiritual journey, back bent and jaw clenched? Yeah, me too. That's why I found Jared C. Wilson's latest book so refreshing. Jared reintroduces readers to the Holy Spirit, exposing the shenanigans perpetrated in his name, while also showing how the Spirit's power is available to every believer for everyday life. If you're hoping for some esoteric knowledge that will elevate you to an elite spiritual status, you'll be disappointed. Jared argues that the Spirit's work isn't spooky or secretive. It's to glorify Jesus and drive us deeper into the heart of the gospel. It's there we find the power we need to live a fruitful, joyful Christian life."

—DREW DYCK, editor at Moody publishers and author of *Yawning at Tigers*

"Jared C. Wilson's gritty, down-to-earth writing style endears itself to gritty, down-to-earth disciples—which is perfect, because that is where most of us find ourselves. I eagerly read this as a means to minister better to others, but suddenly found myself exposed, not only by Jared's Biblical and pastorally shaped insight, but more importantly, by the living and active ministry of the Spirit. On this topic, this has become my new 'go-to' recommendation for everyday followers of Jesus who desire to walk in step with the Spirit."

—CHRIS THOMAS, teaching pastor at Raymond Terrace Community Church, Australia

"As a pastor/church planter, this is the kind of book I've been looking for to put into the hands of my people. It is a book that will help people understand who the Spirit is and demystify a lot of confusion around this topic, while at the same time encouraging them to seek the power of the Holy Spirit. Jared challenges both the hyper-charismatic and the cessationist to find supernatural power in normal, even mundane, everyday living. Jared's trustworthy writing is warm, relatable, and accessible and I would recommend *Supernatural Power for Everyday People* to anyone wanting to know how to live in step with the Spirit as they follow the way of Jesus."

—LUCAS PARKS, lead pastor of Village Church Belfast and director of Acts29 Ireland

"Once again, Jared C. Wilson has written a book that not only serves my own soul, but one that I immediately want to get into the hands of others. If you've ever thought 'there's something missing in my Christian life,' this book will assure you that nothing is missing—except maybe the ongoing awareness of all that God has provided in and through the person and work of his Spirit."

—PETE GREASLEY, pastor of Christchurch, Newport, Wales

"The God of Genesis is truly supernatural, and is capable of so much more than we could ever comprehend. What I appreciate about Jared's book is the careful attention given to God's character, and how he demonstrates that the means of his grace to us are supernatural in and of themselves. In a generation that has been fed lots of content but who often lacks power, all of us need to recognize that we truly need to embrace the supernatural power of the Spirit. It is not limited to charismatic experience, it may be found in the everyday, in the ordinary . . . for what is often masked as ordinary, is truly extraordinary. After all, Christ saved you and me."

—JAY BAUMAN, pastor, director Acts 29 Latin America and Restore Brazil, Rio de Janeiro, Brazil

SUPERNATURAL POWER FOR EVERYDAY PEOPLE

EXPERIENCING GOD'S EXTRAORDINARY
SPIRIT IN YOUR ORDINARY LIFE

JARED C. WILSON

NELSON
BOOKS

An Imprint of Thomas Nelson

Published in Nashville, Tennessee, by Nelson Books, an imprint of Thomas Nelson. Nelson Books and Thomas Nelson are registered trademarks of HarperCollins Christian Publishing, Inc.

Thomas Nelson titles may be purchased in bulk for educational, business, fund-raising, or sales promotional use. For information, please e-mail SpecialMarkets@ThomasNelson.com.

ISBN 978-0-7180-97516 (eBook)

Library of Congress Cataloging-in-Publication Data

ISBN 978-0-7180-97509
Names: Wilson, Jared C., 1975- author.
Title: Supernatural power for everyday people : experiencing God's extraordinary spirit in your ordinary life / by Jared C. Wilson.
Description: Nashville : Thomas Nelson, 2018. | Includes bibliographical references.
Identifiers: LCCN 2017026628 | ISBN 9780718097509
Subjects: LCSH: Holy Spirit. | Christian life. | Supernatural.
Classification: LCC BT121.3 .W55 2018 | DDC 248.4--dc23 LC record available at https://lccn.loc.gov/2017026628

Printed in the United States of America

18 19 20 21 22 LSC 10 9 8 7 6 5 4 3 2

For Ray Ortlund Jr.

CONTENTS

INTRODUCTION

Meet Bill. Bill is twenty-eight years old and lives in a condominium in a typical middle-class suburb of a midsize city. He gets up at 5:30 every morning, shaves, showers, dresses, and eats breakfast. If he has time, he watches some cable news or surfs the web. Forty-five minutes after waking, Bill pours some coffee in a to-go cup and leaves for work.

Bill's commute takes him an hour, sometimes a little more. He tried carpooling once, but he found the carpoolers unreliable, and he knows that if he doesn't leave by 6:15 or so, the traffic will be much thicker and the commute much more frustrating.

Arriving at work around 7:15 (on a good day with no delays), Bill immediately heads to his cubicle. His coworkers are either too busy working or too busy waking up, so nobody gives anybody else much more than a polite nod.

Bill spends four hours pushing numbers around spreadsheets and responding to e-mails.

At lunchtime he walks down to the corner fast-food joint, gets a value meal to go, returns to his cubicle, and eats at his desk while surfing news sites and watching YouTube.

When lunch is over, Bill spends another four to five hours pushing numbers around and responding to e-mails. He takes a few breaks, using the restroom, getting a soda out of the machine in the break room, and playing games on Facebook. Every now and then someone will stop by his cubicle to say hey or chitchat about sports or ask about reports that are due (or *were* due).

At 5:15 p.m., Bill walks out to the parking garage. Some of his coworkers have already left, and the ones who remain are too busy trying to get ready to go home, so nobody holds anybody up. He gets in his car and begins the drive home, which takes longer than the morning commute.

Bill enters his neighborhood at 6:30 p.m., drives to the parking lot of his condo, takes his assigned space, and walks to his front door. He enters the house and turns on the TV. He is too tired to worry about dinner for the moment. At 8:00 p.m. he gets hungry, forages for a can of soup, gets it simmering, and makes a sandwich.

He goes to bed at 11:00, making sure his alarm is set for 5:30 a.m. When the morning comes, he does the same routine all over again.

On Saturdays Bill sometimes goes out, but he mostly stays in and watches movies, plays video games, noodles around on his guitar, and chats with friends on the Internet. On Sunday mornings Bill goes to church, where he is greeted at the door but then talks to no one else. He sits in the same place every week, sings along to the music, usually enjoys the sermon, and goes home immediately after the closing prayer so he doesn't miss the start of the football game.

This is Bill. His life isn't really the kind people write books about, which makes him *totally normal*.

And yet here I am writing a book about people like Bill. Why? Because if there is one thing ordinary people like Bill—and like you and me—need, it's more reminders of just how extraordinary our lives really are.

Does your routine sound a little like Bill's? Maybe it is not as boring or predictable, but it might be just as lonely. Even if Bill were a little older and had a wife and school-aged children, his interaction with them would still be limited because of his daily schedule, and his interaction with those outside his family would be more limited still.

But something happens to Bill. Maybe it's happened to you too. Maybe it's the reason you picked up this book.

One Saturday night Bill finds himself unable to get to sleep. Nothing works. Not tea, not mindless television, not reading, not white noise. They all just remind him of his routine, which reminds him of his routine life, the emptiness of which is what is finally and acutely bothering him.

It's not job stress or relationship fears bothering him at the moment. It's something more vague, more general, and yet somehow keener. A nagging sense of dissatisfaction is keeping Bill awake. He feels as though there must be something more to life, but he's not sure what that could be. He thinks about volunteering at a local homeless shelter, but he isn't sure he has the time. He considers giving more money to charity, but he's not sure he can afford it, and he's not sure he should try to afford it until he pays off all his credit card debt. Every solution Bill thinks of doesn't quite fit the problem that he can't quite define.

It dawns on Bill that his problem may not exactly be something that can be solved by working harder or adding more to his schedule.

When Sunday morning comes, he decides to go to church early and attend a Sunday school class. He sits uneasily through a lesson on Jonah, and when the time comes to share prayer requests, he can hardly contain himself. "I know you don't know me very well," he says to people who don't know him at all. "And I know that I'm a Christian. But I keep feeling like something's missing in my life. I feel like there should be more. I feel lonely, but that's not really the problem. I feel bored, but that's not really the problem. I feel . . ." Bill trails off, trying to think of the right word. Finally, he simply says, "I feel confused."

This is the most Bill has said to anyone in quite a while. And the response from the class isn't very pronounced. A few people nod. A few more shift uneasily in their seats. Bill has broken customary church class protocol, which is mainly oriented around everybody pretending to be fine.

The Sunday school teacher politely says, "Thanks for sharing. Would anyone mind praying for Bill?"

A single woman named Carrie agrees to pray for Bill, and in just a few short lines she asks that God would give Bill peace, comfort, wisdom, and a sense of God's own divine presence.

Not much happens. Bill wasn't quite sure what to ask for and nobody was quite sure what to pray for. The class quickly moves on to the next prayer request, and afterward Bill walks to the auditorium for the worship service.

But now something different happens. He sings the songs a little louder. He listens a little more intently to the sermon. When it's over, his drive home feels less lonely. Nobody gave him any religious homework. Nobody even gave him an answer! But for some reason he feels suddenly more . . . *joyful*.

Bill has experienced something new, something fresh from

the Spirit of God. It makes him feel a certain way, sure, but it's not simply about feelings. What he feels is really more of an assurance—a *re*assurance—that he is rooted to something deeper than his feelings, something bigger than the earthly agendas and ambitions of his everyday life.

He was not able to put it this way at the time, but what he experienced was actually what the apostle Paul talked about in Romans 8:16—the Holy Spirit of God testifying to his own spirit that he belonged to the Father.

And this is just the tip of the spiritual iceberg. Every Christian is vitally connected to the person and work of the Spirit of the living God! And we experience this connection in a variety of ways, ways that are reflective of the Spirit's divine nature and power.

I am firmly convinced that too many Christians spend most of their lives trying to carry out their everyday routines in their own strength. The Bible has lots of warnings about this precisely because it's such a common tendency. It just comes naturally to us.

But followers of Jesus Christ have someone supernatural living right inside their very spirits. Anyone who has repented of sin and exercised faith in Jesus, in fact, has done so because of the supernatural power of the Holy Spirit. And this power takes up residence in our lives for all eternity. God has "set up shop," as it were, in our hearts. Discovering this extraordinary, life-changing reality is what this book is all about.

I've known lots of Bills throughout my time in church communities. Heck, more than a few times, I've *been* Bill. One day I feel numb to my routine, like a zombie on a treadmill, just going through the required motions, wondering if anything I am doing matters or is amounting to anything. Then, for some reason I can't quite put my finger on, I have a bit more *oomph*. My routine didn't change, but my vision seems a little clearer, my steps firmer, my future brighter, even if still unknown.

You could chalk this up to some kind of mood swing or the rise and fall in one's seasonal affective disorder. In Bill's case, you could argue that just being able to talk to somebody helped lift his mood. There is no doubt these are important factors in the complex dispositions of human nature. But for the Christian there is something else. There is in fact *someone* else.

In my capacity as a pastor, I have had many conversations with people walking weary miles in Bill's worn shoes. In the early years of my ministry, I would have tried every kind of pep talk I could think of to cheer them up. But as time went on and I gathered more experience (and by God's grace, more wisdom), I came to believe that most Christians struggling with purpose and vision and boredom and powerlessness didn't really need more things to do or better catchphrases on which to hang their hopes. What they needed was a peek behind the curtain to the reality of their inner lives.

CHAPTER 1

THE PROBLEM WITH YOUR INNER LIFE

Experiencing the Spirit's Conviction

Apart from God's power, there is no Christian life. This crucial truth makes the phrase "Christian life in the power of the Spirit" essentially redundant. The Holy Spirit causes the process that Jesus referred to as "being born again," and the Holy Spirit seals those who are born again to ensure they stand blameless before God at the end of their days, and the Holy Spirit sustains those who are born again every millisecond between those two moments. Because of this, if a person lived apart from the power of the Holy Spirit, he would not be a Christian—in fact, he could not even be said to be spiritually alive at all!

But many of us—Christians included—don't think of God's power this way. We experience an especially powerful church service and say things like, "God showed up!" We muddle through an extended period of spiritual drought and say, "God is hiding from me" or "God is giving me the silent treatment right now." We read in some books or hear in some sermons that God really wants to bless us in some exceptional way if we would only "let" him. All of these ways of thinking betray a fundamental misunderstanding of God's real presence in our daily lives.

We need to understand that when our life feels lacking in power, it's not because we haven't actualized our innate potential. In fact, that's the problem! When our life is lacking in power, it's typically because we are working in our own strength too much!

Similarly, when our life is lacking vision and we feel confused and bored, it's not because we are missing out on the power of positive thinking—it's precisely *because* we are leaning on our own understanding.

When Christians live sluggish Christian lives, it's not because they don't have enough of God but because they have too much of themselves. Because, in actuality, it is impossible for any true Christian not to have enough God.

If you are a Christian—that is, if you are someone who has repented of your sins and placed your faith in Jesus Christ alone for salvation—God's presence in your life is guaranteed. His love is always over you, his Son in heaven is always interceding for you, and his Spirit has taken up residence in your soul to give you the power required for every need you have.

This is God's honest truth.

And yet too many of us live weak, pitiful Christian lives. We constantly feel spiritually dry, theologically confused, and religiously weary. Is there any hope for us?

It's not as if we aren't looking for answers. It's just that we too often look for these answers in the wrong places. Or, alternatively, when we incline our ear to reliable sources of truth, we misunderstand what they're saying. The first mistake we make is looking inside ourselves for the help we need. We won't find the solution in the place where the problem is.

If we want to participate in the truly supernatural life in this earthly world, we have to stop looking for earthly solutions to our problems.

The First Step Is Realizing You Don't Have What It Takes

Once upon a time, my friend Ray and I each planted a church. We planted our churches in the same year in the same place. In fact, the church I planted met on Sunday evenings in Ray's church building. On some Sunday mornings, some folks from my church would attend Ray's church. We really enjoyed Ray's preaching, and we wanted to be the kind of encouragement to his church plant that they had been to us.

My church plant was attended almost exclusively by young people. My wife and I were probably the oldest people in the church. Ray's church plant was attended almost exclusively by old people. When we attended Ray's church services, we brought their average age down quite a bit!

I remember going to some of those early church services and feeling sorry for Ray. *He's such a great preacher*, I thought. *He really deserves to have more than a handful of blue-haired old ladies in his church.*

Now, I have nothing against blue-haired old ladies. In fact, having since pastored a church with a vibrant contingent of old folks in it, I can attest to the fact that blue-haired old ladies are often the sweetest, most encouraging people you can have in a church! But my vision was dull. I was leaning on my own understanding. I was looking at Ray's church and wondering how in the world it was going to "work." I mean, there's a reason nobody in the missional world is planting Blue-Haired Old Lady Community Church in your local neighborhood!

Well, I have to tell you that my church plant doesn't exist anymore. We regrettably had to close its doors when God called my wife and me to a ministry in another state.

Ray's church? Well, I happened to be back in town on the Sunday they were celebrating their fifth anniversary. The place was full. All the blue-haired old ladies were still there. In fact, aside from a couple of folks who had passed away, all the founding members were still there. But they had also seen hundreds of other believers of every generation and multiple races join their ranks. I don't know if I've ever been happier to feel like an idiot.

I remember Ray sharing these words with the congregation on that anniversary morning: "God's been very gracious to us. People ask me how this church has grown. I think we've seen such sweet growth because none of us showed up five years ago with big ideas and visionary plans. We were all weak. Some of us were hurt. Some of us were confused. But we all came here broken. And the Lord can use that."

The apostle Paul spoke of this dynamic this way:

> But he said to me, "My grace is sufficient for you, for my power is made perfect in weakness." Therefore I will boast all the more gladly of my weaknesses, so that the power of Christ may rest upon me. For the sake of Christ, then, I am content with

weaknesses, insults, hardships, persecutions, and calamities. For when I am weak, then I am strong (2 Cor. 12:9–10).

These important truths follow Paul's sharing of one of the greatest pains of his life. He had a "thorn in the flesh" that had been afflicting him constantly, and he had pleaded with God to take it away. We don't know exactly what this thorn was, but it appears to have been a kind of spiritual oppression that caused him extreme physical and psychological discomfort. These are not the kinds of feelings we typically equate with a victorious Christian life! And yet for Paul this pain was the entryway to experiencing God's power, because it was precisely this pain that kept him at the end of himself and totally reliant on the Holy Spirit.

Even without being able to articulate it, this is what Bill was tapping into in that Sunday school class. He was finally able to confess his utter confusion—his weakness—and this admission prompted his calling out to God for help. This is certainly the reality that Ray was acknowledging in his church planter testimony.

I love that Ray's church has even adopted this reality as their official "mantra," which goes like this: "I'm a complete idiot. My future's incredibly bright. Anyone can get in on this."[1]

So, yes, contrary to the teaching of so many self-help gurus and religious motivational speakers, the key to empowered living is acknowledging that *we don't have what it takes*. The key to living a victorious Christian life is first understanding that we are losers. Our inner human potential is only a mediocre help compared to what we truly need. And we possess no innate virtue that can bring us lasting joy, peace, and hope. Our innate nature in fact is sinful and deceitful.

This is why the things we so often do to compensate for our experience of weakness only exacerbate it.

The Failure of Our Compartmentalized Lives

One of Bill's problems is that he mistakes the behavioral tidiness and normalcy of his routine for spiritual tidiness and normalcy. But he has fallen into the trap that is all too common in our modern lives. He has compartmentalized his spirituality.

What I mean is, Bill has begun to think of his spirituality as just one aspect of his life, perhaps referred to as his Religious Self. Monday through Friday Bill is living the life of his Vocational Self (what many of us think of simply as our Normal Self). On Saturday, then, he lives the life of his Recreational Self. When Sunday comes, it's time for Bill to become his Religious Self.

The Vocational Self goes to work, eats meals, pays bills, and does the regular mundane tasks thought necessary to well-adjusted adulthood. The Recreational Self is how we compensate for the stress of spending time as our Vocational Self—the reward we give ourselves for paying the dues of our Vocational Self. Then we become our Religious Self on the days or in the moments when we feel especially needful of a higher power or simply when we feel the need to access our "spirituality."

Each version of ourselves resides in its own neat compartment, stays in its own lane. It's rare for us to access multiple versions of ourselves at the same moment. It's as if we think of our inner life as a boardroom table occupied by multiple employees—directors, if you will, of our multiple responsibilities or interests. Around the table we divvy up workloads and time commitments to our Normal Self, our Recreational Self, our Religious Self. We may even have slots assigned to Family and Friends and Education. Our system feels very coherent and cohesive. But in fact, it is quite disjointed and divided.

I knew that someone in my church was trying to live a compartmentalized life when she would say things like, "I just don't have much time for God these days." Or when he'd say theologically confused things like, "I guess I just need to trust in my faith more" (which is basically like saying, "I need to have trust in my trust").

You know that someone is living a compartmentalized life when their social media bio includes a Bible verse but their photos display them unashamedly engaged in all kinds of things the Bible forbids or warns against. I have been utterly confused to see friends or fellow churchgoers posting sexually suggestive photos, images of themselves binge drinking, or graphics featuring quotes full of profanity or perversity, and right there in their profiles sits Jeremiah 29:11 or Philippians 4:13. I had to "unfollow" one young lady who attended my church because she had the inexplicable habit of posting sexy selfies of herself with Bible verses or inspirational Christian quotes in the captions. This is just one real-life example of what the Bible calls being "double-minded" (James 1:8; 4:8).

The man secretly indulging in his porn addiction while constantly complaining about gay marriage is living a compartmentalized life. The woman who neglects her kids to spend hours and hours on the Internet blogging about how to be a better mom is living a compartmentalized life. The pastor who preaches against drunkenness and lack of self-control on Sundays then goes home and eats like a glutton the rest of the week and engages in arguments on social media is living a compartmentalized life.

The "power problem" with this way of living should be somewhat obvious. If we assign God and his Word a *portion* of our lives, we are at the same time seeking to detach the other portions from his sovereign power. This is what the Bible calls "quenching the Spirit."

The compartmentalized approach promises to make our lives easier, more manageable. But anytime we try to make areas of our lives off-limits to God's authority or to the Holy Spirit's prompting, we find the rest of our lives given to greater and greater messiness.

The most significant practical issue with compartmentalized living is that our Religious Self inevitably becomes our smallest self. Many Christians say they believe in the God of the universe and have trusted in the Son of God as their Lord and Savior but then spend the bulk of their lives obeying other lords and trusting other saviors.

When we relegate our intentionality with God to a minute fraction of our time, it's no wonder we feel distant from him during the times we happen to be thinking about him and lack power during all the other times. Whatever we focus most of our conscious time on will invariably dominate the way we think and feel.

That Nagging Sense of Emptiness Is a Gift

We should probably stop picking on poor old Bill, but we need to help him see that his life revolves around his own agenda, his own needs, his own wants. It's not good that his spiritual life is compartmentalized, fit into the larger order of his "normal" lifestyle. Bill has arranged things to be as convenient as possible, and even when he has the inclination to "do hard things," he is usually too tired to do them. Bill is not often faced with the opportunity to serve or help others because he rarely makes time to interact with others in substantive ways. It is hard for him to be generous with others because he is generally generous with himself and thinks of others as window dressing in his life. And over time just doing the regular, ordinary, mundane, "easy" things of life seems to take more and more out of Bill because he has cordoned them off from his only hope for minute-by-minute power.

Every message Bill takes in only reinforces his problem as it promises to alleviate it. His environment and its "gospel" keep sending him further into himself, which is where all his issues began in the first place.

This is not the way God has designed life to be lived.

So what's the answer? What is poor old Bill to do?

The first thing he ought to do is recognize that this sense of longing, this nagging sense of emptiness, is itself a gift! It is, in fact, something God is doing. God is speaking to him. He has led Bill right into his own Ecclesiastes, where he will realize, as King Solomon did, that all the comings and goings and doings and earnings can never satisfy the eternity in his heart (Eccl. 3:11).

This realization of dissatisfaction is a severe mercy from God himself. It is a mercy because the worst thing that might happen to us is to be completely content and happy apart from experiencing the power of God. No, this nagging sense of dissatisfaction is a gift of the Spirit, a form in fact of the Spirit's conviction of us over our sin. We all ought to beg the Spirit to make us dissatisfied when we are distracted from God and neglecting our worship of him.

In fact, anytime any human being is dealing with utter emptiness and lack of fulfillment in life, it is the result of the God-embedded message inside that the person needs God. The Holy Spirit who separates order from chaos is warning that person about life apart from his power.

And when we listen, that is the Spirit's power working too.

Bill is listening. And so it's time for Bill to head to the boardroom of his interior life and fire all those other directors. He needs to give every employee a pink slip. He needs to let them know that their services are no longer required. Then he needs to go out into the office space of his life and knock down all the cubicle walls with extreme prejudice. He needs to vanquish the compartments of his inner life. He has experienced the Spirit's conviction, which has primed him to experience the Spirit's power.

Maybe you need to follow Bill's lead. Maybe you need to wave the white flag. While submitting to the Spirit's conviction may seem to promise less control, less security, it is instead the way to maximize the power available to every square inch of your life. You will now be surrendering the eight-lane highway of your life to the free rein of the Spirit of the living God. His joy will now spill over into every compartment. And when you expose more and more of your inner life to the otherworldly message of God, his power will spill over into your *outer* life too.

This power is what Jesus Christ has promised you.

CHAPTER 2

THE PROMISE OF MYSTERIOUS POWER

Experiencing the Spirit's Presence

Do you ever wonder why we don't see the kinds of miracles today that we see in the Bible? I'm sure this thought has occurred to you at least once or twice. Maybe you don't think too much about it, but it's a question that has come up frequently in my own life.

When I was a child hearing all the fantastic things taking place in the Bible stories—fire falling from heaven, water turning to blood, paralyzed men walking—I always wondered why God didn't seem to do those same things today. My favorite miracle story when I was a child was Jesus' feeding of the five thousand. We were always told that the boy brought to Jesus in John 6 with his little bit of bread and fish had been the only one sent to hear Jesus with a lunch box in hand, packed by his thoughtful mom. Clearly, mom-centered propaganda! But I always found that story staggering. I wondered how Jesus did it. How did he take a fish sandwich (basically) and turn it into a meal for five thousand people, with baskets of leftovers? Yes, *by his power.* But what did he physically do? Did he keep pulling food out of a never-emptying basket? Did he just keep tearing morsels off of never-diminishing bread and fish? I was fascinated. And it made me believe that miracles were always just around the corner.

As I got older, of course, this sense of miraculous antici-pation diminished. I prayed for girlfriends I didn't get. I prayed to pass tests that I failed. I prayed for big muscles. No dice. Jesus didn't seem to come through on my mundane requests very often; I wasn't really expecting him to show up in the comparatively more extraordinary signs and wonders.

And then the question changed. The wording was still the same, but the intention behind it was different. "Why doesn't God do miracles today like he did in the Bible?" didn't fuel wonder so much as skepticism. My period of wrestling with the reliability of the Bible and the veracity of the Christian faith it teaches was, by God's grace, thankfully brief. I don't recall ever really having a crisis of faith where outright belief in God hung in the balance. But I certainly wrestled from time to time with whether what the Bible said happened actually happened. Maybe, like some of the "experts" said, the Bible wasn't true in the historical sense but true in other ways.

Later the miracles question became less about intellectual skepticism and more about theological curiosity. I believed soon enough—and still do—that the events depicted in the Scriptures as historical accounts were historically accurate and that the Bible could be trusted to report events as they had really happened, including all the crazy stuff about living people being sucked up into heaven, frightened people walking through parted seas, and fortunate people hearing the very voice of God. So the question from my childhood remained: Why doesn't God do this stuff anymore? Why don't we see these same kinds of signs and wonders in our modern age?

You Don't Need Miracles

I don't know if my answers to these questions will satisfy you. I don't know if they completely satisfy *me*! I have learned, spending most of my middle-aged life following Jesus, that sometimes the only answer God gives us to our questions is, "You don't need to know that." The older I get, the more satisfied I am with that kind of response from God. But I think we have some answers to these questions in the Bible itself.

You'll notice, for instance, that in the New Testament the miracles become less and less *grandiose*—for lack of a better word—when Jesus begins his ministry. The heaven-dispensed wonders playing out on the large stage of nature seem to fade away, and the miracles become more *personal*. Yes, Jesus does things like turning water into wine and walking on the sea, but most of his miracles are healings of individuals. The biggest miracle in the New Testament is of course the resurrection of Jesus Christ himself, precipitated by his miraculous raisings of Lazarus, Jairus's daughter, and the widow's son at Nain. There were also signs in the heavens when Jesus was crucified, and the heavy curtain in the temple was miraculously torn in two.

These exceptions are important, but I think anyone familiar

with the entire story line of the Bible will recognize that the kind of miracles appearing in the New Testament are largely different from those appearing in the Old Testament.[1] As the Christian narrative takes off, we have the wonder at Pentecost (which we'll return to later) and the ensuing miracles attending the mission of the apostles of the early church. They perform some remarkable signs, but again, most of them remain on the personal level, and as the book of Acts progresses, and as the testimony of the early church unfolds in the historical record found after the Bible, we see them less and less.

Some people believe miraculous signs (and the so-called charismatic gifts) ceased after the death of the last apostle or at the closing of the canon. Some believe they may continue today but occur more often in places where Christianity is new, just as in the days of New Testament Christianity, signifying the inbreaking of the kingdom among unreached peoples. Others say miracles could be just as common today as they were back then if only we had enough faith and weren't so enamored with modernity.

Scholars suggest all kinds of reasons why we don't experience the same sort of miraculous faith as our biblical forefathers, but this is not a scholarly book and I don't care to give you scholarly answers.

And besides, you don't need miracles.

Too many of us spend our Christian lives waiting on something big to happen, completely oblivious to the fact that the biggest thing that could ever happen to us already did, and it's more than enough. In fact, to be greedy for something more is to suggest that what's been given is somehow deficient.

Craving more and more extravagant evidences of the Spirit

is an easy way to demonstrate our lack of satisfaction with the gospel of Jesus. No work of the Spirit, in fact, can be as big or as glorious as the work of converting our hearts to Jesus. So if our spiritual appetites are constantly set on more, we may find ourselves, ironically, experiencing *less*, even if something extraordinary happens to us.

There was one time in my life when I experienced what some people call being "slain in the Spirit." I don't know how else to categorize it; it's the only named phenomenon that seems to describe what happened to me. I was in student ministry at the time, and we had taken the youth for a camp week in Estes Park, Colorado. You should know up front that our church was not a charismatic church, and I was not a charismatic believer. Far from it, on both counts. Our youth group did not have any prior experience with any of the stuff you may see at churches where charismatic experiences are said to take place: nobody spoke in tongues, nobody attempted public healings, nobody was trying to cast out demons, nobody was doing the kind of altar call ministry that involves people shaking, falling, spinning, or shouting. In fact, culturally and corporately, we would have repudiated all those things. We were Baptist, dang it.

Our camp speaker was an itinerant preacher named Todd. He preached clear, blunt, biblical sermons. Like most Baptist churches did at the time, we conducted response times at the end of messages, but Todd did not conduct them in the "heads bowed, eyes closed" manner we were used to. "Heads up, eyes open," I remember him saying. "If you won't stand up for Christ in a room full of Christians, you certainly won't stand up for him in the world." I would do things differently today, but I still appreciate that approach.

In any event, the point is that we did not seek to facilitate anything crazy or charismatic. But something happened anyway.

As we sang a worship song at the close of the service that night, the Lord came down. I don't really even like that phrase, but I don't know how else to describe what happened. There was a palpable sense of the presence of God in that room unlike any I'd ever experienced. I was so overcome with the sense of God's presence that I realized I couldn't stay in the room, that something was happening to me, and I needed to remove myself because I didn't want to be a distraction to anyone. I didn't even know what was happening, but I didn't want to take anyone's attention away from worship.

I left my seat and made my way to the back of the room. With each step, I could feel more and more a sense of love filling me. I know even that sounds vague—a sense of love?—but that's what it was. I exited the gathering room, entering the main part of the conference center, and I just kept walking. I wanted to go outside. I had no sooner passed through the inner glass doors, entering a little tiled entryway separated from the cool Colorado night by another set of glass doors, when I was—well, I guess *tackled* might be the right word. I was knocked down by something invisible. I was taken to the floor by an unseen force. It wasn't violent. I wasn't in pain. In fact, I was overwhelmed by an engulfing sense of peace and comfort, a sense of ecstasy, something like a warm electric current. The sensation was soothing. I didn't shake or convulse. I didn't yell anything or froth at the mouth. I didn't erupt in fits of "holy laughter" or—worse—animal noises, phenomena rising to some prominence at the time, thanks to the reports of alleged revivals in Toronto and Brownsville, Florida. No, but I was happy. Very, very happy. And I couldn't get up. I was held down. It felt like something or someone was hugging me to the ground.

Nobody saw me, as far as I know. This experience did not occur before an audience. And after about ninety seconds, I was able to stand up. I went outside, still reeling. The Rocky Mountains against the night sky looked more vivid than any sight I'd ever seen. I was in love with God. I believed he had done something exceptional, something *extra* for me. Why? I don't know. I'd always been a neurotic, insecure young man, and if I had to guess, I would suppose the Lord—since that's who I believe did this—was just writing a momentary exclamation point on his love for me.

But I wasn't the only one who experienced God's extraordinary outpouring of love. Students began filing outside, eyes wide open and big smiles on their faces. They were singing and praying, and some of them were jumping up and down. Let me reiterate that this wasn't something that had ever happened before in this church. It wasn't something we had ever encouraged or suggested. If anything, we would have discouraged what felt kooky. But God was ministering to us in a different way. One boy walked up to me, a huge grin on his face, and asked, "What's happening to us?"

"I don't know," I replied.

Nothing like that ever happened to me again. Oh, I've had some emotional responses to preaching and music in worship services. That happens quite frequently, I must confess. I'm kind of a sap, especially when I'm reminded of God's grace for me. But I've never experienced anything close to that "slain in the Spirit" moment.

I'm glad it happened. But I've never longed for that experience.

I haven't sought it out. I haven't asked God to do it again. If he wants to, I'm game. But it's not normal. And that's okay. This is why:

We already have power, amazing power.

In fact, most of the Bible—the parts where outrageous signs and wonders aren't being performed—suggests to us that what believers in Jesus have is actually *better* than miracles.

Heaven in Your Heart

I'm not sure if you've read the Bible lately, but the things it says are astounding, outrageous. In fact, I find most of the Bible's theological assertions even more mind-blowing than its miraculous events!

First of all, just the fact that we have this Bible is itself a monumental thing. That ordinary men would be inspired by God to capture the breath of God into a book is staggering. The Bible is like lightning in a bottle. The great poet George Herbert said that the Bible is "heaven laid flat."[2] You open up this book, and heaven is there.

When I read 2 Peter 1:3–4, for instance, it feels like heaven to me. Everything I need to know and experience to escape death and participate in the very life and nature of the triune God is in this passage. And I think even that undersells it. Take a look:

His divine power has granted to us all things that pertain to life and godliness, through the knowledge of him who called us to his own glory and excellence, by which he has granted to us his precious and very great promises, so that through them you may become partakers of the divine nature, having escaped from the corruption that is in the world because of sinful desire.

What Peter was describing here makes the good advice dispensed by many churches and their teachers seem very, very shallow. This passage is a blowtorch to sentimental religious pick-me-ups.

See, here is the problem with good advice. It doesn't go deep enough. It's sort of like this: If you wanted to put a highway tunnel through a mountain, and you put some dynamite on the face of that mountain, you might end up moving some stone, but you'd really just be taking off some layers. But if you were to drill down deep into the mountain and put the dynamite inside of it, the explosion would be much more effective.

Well, 2 Peter 1:3–4 is dynamite set deep down into the heart—right down in the nerve center where we seek to manage the compartments of our lives. Remember, as we learned in chapter 1, the problem with us is not simply that we have to deal with negativity in the world. The problem with us is that we have a deep, deep well of negativity already inside of us. The problem is our inner life, not just our outer behavior. And it's worse than negativity; it's sin. The storm of cosmic rebellion is raging inside our souls.

What 2 Peter 1:3–4 offers is not just better than good advice; it is better than miraculous signs! What Peter was touching on here is something eternally powerful—power *straight out of heaven*—to put down in the recesses of our hearts. "His divine power has granted to us all things that pertain to life and godliness."

This is the biggest of big deals, evidenced implicitly by just how eager Peter was to get this information out! This is the opening of his letter; he had just started his greeting, and already he was bursting with good news. No chitchat. Just a quick hello and then, *boom*, "divine power."

He didn't ask, "So how are you guys? You doing okay?" No, he said, "Hello. Grace to you. His divine power has granted to us all things that pertain to life and godliness."

Do you have a friend who can't stay on the surface, and you sometimes find that annoying? You're just trying to talk about sports, and this guy's always interrupting with something like, "I'll tell you what, the Christian life is no game, man."

What?

Or you try to talk about the weather: "They say it's going to rain pretty good tomorrow." And this guy's saying things like, "Well, my Lord Jesus Christ is gonna be reigning for all eternity."

Do you know that guy?

Well, Peter was that guy. He couldn't even get through his greeting without preaching the gospel (but if you know anything about Peter's testimony, you might understand why): "His divine power has granted to us all things that pertain to life and godliness."

What is it that you and I need in both the storms of life and the ordinary boredom of life? Not good advice and not inspirational pick-me-ups. No, we need *power*. We need real power.

When life is falling apart, when we don't feel like we can go on, when the bottom has dropped out, when we feel the creeping darkness of doubt or despair, when we're constantly battling sin—we need power.

And when life is going normally, when the routines have become way too routine, when each day blends into the next, when the only concern you have is that vague, nagging sense that "there has to be more than this"—you need power.

Motivational pick-me-ups only last so long. What we need is power. And Peter was saying that *divine* power has been *granted* to us.

What for?

For "all things" pertaining to life and godliness. All things. There are no loopholes here. No asterisks. God is not holding out on us. When we feel like he is, it's often because our hopes are set on the wrong outcomes. We want relief from pain or pressure, and he's granting relief from the greatest threat we spend most of our lives not thinking about—the threat of damnation.

It turns out, after all, that our desire for miracles is a setting of our sights too low, not too high. While you may not be itching to see a miraculous vision or experience a wondrous suspension of the laws of nature or receive some kind of heavenly directed financial windfall, most of us lapse into this "waiting on a sign" kind of Christian life far too often. You and I engage every day in our own personal versions of the prosperity gospel.

Oh, I know, you don't send money for the televangelist's private jet, but you engage in another kind of prosperity gospel every day. And so do I. We are constantly looking for people and things other than God and his glory to satisfy us, to give us what we want. To give us what we *think* we need. We are looking for signs and consequently missing the truth that we already have what the signs have been pointing to all along.

We think, *If I try hard enough, if I do well enough, if I just accomplish this or achieve that, then I will finally be satisfied.* And it never works, does it? It never works because the things we're trusting in don't work. But they also never work because the things we're trying to satisfy usually aren't our biggest problems. Most of us just want health and security. Meanwhile, God wants to rescue us from corruption and condemnation and reconcile us to himself as beloved children of the King.

Our souls are dry from sin and striving, and we're in the oasis of the world drinking up more sand.

Then God comes down with living water. And so we have divine power for life. But also divine power for godliness! The same gospel power that justifies us also sanctifies us (1 Cor. 6:11). The same power that regenerates us now counsels and convicts us and leads us into all truth. The same glory that demands we be holy begins to make us holy!

If you're like me, when you hear all this, you're thinking, *Well, okay. I'll have that. How do I get it?*

Well, this is how Peter said that God has granted us by his divine power everything that pertains to life and godliness: "Through the knowledge of him who called us to his own glory and excellence." He was saying that knowing Jesus is the antidote to death and sinfulness. Life and godliness come through knowing Jesus. And Jesus, like his Father, is not stingy with his gifts. The Father says, "I want these ungrateful rebels, these rotting spiritual corpses, to have *everything* that pertains to life and godliness." So the Son says, "Well, then, I'll call them into my glory and excellence."

Sounds like a plan.

This is why Jesus didn't simply show up with a set of religious instructions or some spiritual advice. The people he came to already had that. No, he showed up with salvation. And this salvation is deep. It goes back to before the earth was a gleam in the Father's eye, and it goes forward into the endless days of the new heaven and new earth. Salvation is infinitely deep.

Before time began, God was looking forward through the time and space he had yet to create, and he saw you and your inevitable sin and said, "I want that one."

That's astounding.

The depths of wonder here are deeper than any miraculous sign, more fascinating than any spectacular wonder, more exhilarating than any momentary spiritual thrill. Walking on the waves is a miracle, but the gospel is the ocean.

We get a sense of this here just in the way Peter made this claim. Can you untangle this?

> His divine power grants us "all things" through Christ.
>> Being in Christ means being called to his glory and excellence.
>> Being called to his glory and excellence means being granted precious and great promises (which refer to the abundance of eternal blessings we receive as children of God).
>> Being granted precious and great promises means partaking of the divine nature.

Unbelievable. The further we go, the deeper we get—the more beauty, the more wonder, the more glory there is to be had, all by God's grace, and given to us in Spiritual power.*

I am reminded of 2 Corinthians 3:18, where Paul said it is by

---

* I often capitalize the word *Spiritual* when referring specifically to a work of God's Holy Spirit. When simply referring to a "spiritual sense" or our "spiritual life," I will keep the word lowercase. This is a small way I seek to remind myself and you that what we receive from God spiritually is a work of the Holy Spirit, whom we should not neglect or ignore.

beholding the glory of Christ that we are "transformed . . . from one degree of glory to another."

Receiving the glory of Jesus changes us. This is why the gospel cannot be boring. It declares and imparts the glory of Christ. If you find the gospel less interesting than miraculous signs, it is only because you do not see how surpassingly wonderful the gospel is! The gospel cannot get boring any more than Jesus can get boring.

And I don't know about you, but Peter's use of the phrase "you may become partakers of the divine nature" really freaks me out. What does that even mean?

Well, I don't rightly know, but like George Herbert has suggested, it feels like heaven laid flat. Becoming a partaker of God's divine nature certainly doesn't sound like religious business as usual.

And it doesn't simply sound like theological knowledge. The thing about theological knowledge is that it becomes deceptively easy, because of the sin in us, to equate our spiritual strength with what we know *about* God. But even the demons know *about* God. And the demons can knock you down on the floor too if they really want to. Even Pharaoh's magicians were able to re-create some of Moses' miracles. But one miracle the enemy can't perform is this: he can't make you a partaker of the divine nature.

No, Peter wasn't talking about simply knowing more about God. That's a start, but it's not the whole. What Peter was talking about is *actually knowing* God. "You may become partakers of the divine nature" is thrilling in a mysterious way.

I think of the conversion of perhaps the greatest American preacher of all time, Jonathan Edwards, who was minding his own religious business one day when 1 Timothy 1:17 fell into his soul. This is what Edwards said:

> The first instance that I remember of that sort of inward, sweet delight in God and divine things that I have lived much in since, was on reading those words, 1 Tim. 1:17, "Now unto the King, eternal, immortal, invisible, the only wise God, be honor and glory forever and ever, Amen." As I read the words, there came into my soul, and was as it were diffused through it, a sense of the glory of the Divine Being; a new sense, quite different from any thing I ever experienced before. Never any words of Scripture seemed to me as these words did. I thought with myself, how excellent a Being that was, and how happy I should be, if I might enjoy that God, and be rapt up to him in heaven; and be as it were swallowed up in him for ever![3]

This is what 2 Peter 1:4 does for me as well. I'm "a partaker of the divine nature," and that's too wonderful for me! It is frightening and freeing and too wonderful! I want to be "swallowed up in God."

And in a way, what Peter was saying is that *we are* swallowed up in God.

Second Peter 1:3–4 calls us to a deeper and yet simultaneously higher reality that makes our religious effort the outflow of being connected on a soul level to the God of the universe.

I'm uncomfortable even writing that, because God is holy and just and mighty and powerful—and I am not. He is the God of Abraham and Isaac and Jacob. He speaks reality into existence. He makes the earth his footstool. He stirs up oceans with his finger. He holds the universe in the palm of his hand like it's a dainty glass figurine. He is the Alpha and Omega, the beginning and the end. He is the great I AM, Yahweh, the one true God. And here Peter was saying that his power—which gives us Christ, which gives us glory, which gives us promises—gives us a participation of some kind in the very life of God.

This is too wonderful. We have to tread lightly here. We have to take off our shoes.

Now, we're not talking about becoming God or gods or anything like that. Rather, as Edwards wrote about 2 Peter 1:4, we "are made partakers of God's fullness . . . that is, of God's spiritual beauty and happiness, according to the measure and capacity of a creature."4 Put another way, we don't partake of the *essence* of God—his divinity—but of the *nature* of God—his holiness and joy and "all things that pertain to life and godliness."

This is a serious and weighty thing. And it is a wonderful and exhilarating thing. To become a partaker of the divine nature is to discover how delicious the grace of God in Christ really is and—this is important and crucial and a natural consequence of tasting God's goodness—*losing our taste for the things of the world.*

This was where Peter was going. We have *all of this* "having escaped from the corruption that is in the world because of sinful desire."

Now, I don't know about you, but this gives me an entirely new perspective on my everyday life than I am naturally accustomed to having.

The next time someone asks you, "How are you doing?" you say, "Are you kidding? I'm a partaker of the divine nature of God! How are you?" It's certainly a lot better than "Too blessed to be stressed."

Second Peter 1:3–4 helps us in every moment, because if you have repented of your sin and trusted in Christ's finished work on the cross and out of the tomb, in every moment, no matter where you are or what you're doing, you are united to Christ. You are partaking in the fullness of his beauty and greatness.

This is how you escape the corruption of the sinful desire confronting you on that computer screen.

This is how you escape the lure of comparing yourself to others around you.

This is how you stop hating people and envying people and treating people poorly.

Second Peter 1:3–4 is how you know you aren't lost! That you haven't slipped through the cracks. That you aren't forgotten or forsaken.

About thirteen years ago, seven years after my "slain in the Spirit" experience, I spent every night for weeks facedown on the floor of our guest bedroom, groaning to God to help me, to save me from depressive thoughts of grief and pain. I was intermittently suicidal, full of despair. Sometimes I just repeated one word over and over: "Please . . . please . . . please. . . ."

And the Lord reached down from heaven and in an extraordinary way one evening spoke to my heart in a still, small voice with a powerful, enormous impact: "I love you and I approve of you."

I know he didn't love the sins I'd committed that had contributed to my devastation, and I know he didn't approve of me on my own, but he was making precious and very great promises to me that by his grace I had been hidden with his Son in himself (Col. 3:3).

The power I tapped into that night was the same power that had tackled me years earlier in that conference center doorway in the Rocky Mountains. It is a power I have every single morning that I open my eyes and take my first waking breath, whether I'm conscious of it or not. And it is a power that I have every night when I'm not conscious at all.

But if you want to "tap into" this power with me, we have to stop talking about it like it's an *it* in the first place.

No Such *Thing* as the Holy Spirit

We don't have to venture too far into the world of religious resources today to find writers and leaders, songwriters and singers, even pastors and preachers treating the power—that ostensibly comes from God—like "it's" some kind of impersonal force, some kind of biblical fairy dust that we can use, dispense, or otherwise manipulate. Heck, I even used the phrase "tap into" in the previous paragraph. We see it in any Christian talk that refers to our supposed ability to "unleash" or "activate" the Spirit, or anytime we talk about "letting God" do something. A few famous preachers on social media routinely suggest to their audiences that unless they pray, obey, or engage in other positive actions, "God can't" bless them.

The cumulative effect of all this kind of talk is the overwhelming—and overwhelmingly bad—suggestion that the power of God is some kind of force, like in Star Wars. But this line of spiritual thinking owes more to Far Eastern mysticism and New Age occultism than biblical Christianity. Indeed, what we see in the hyper-charismatic events depicted on televangelist programs and what we read in the Twitter feeds of the prosperity gospelists is more like witchcraft than Christianity.

The power that Peter said makes us partakers of God's divine nature is not some impersonal force. In fact, it is not an *it* at all. This power is the very presence of God himself in our lives, the presence of God's Holy Spirit.

What is the Holy Spirit?

Again: not what. *Who.* The Holy Spirit is the third person of the triune God, coequally and coeternally God along with the Father and the Son. He is omnipotent, omniscient, and omnipresent. As God, he has always existed, and he always will. He proceeds from the Father and the Son, though he shares the same essential nature they do. Equal with both the Father and the Son, he is commissioned by the Father to glorify the Son and apply the work of the Son to the lives of believers.

I am sorry if that is getting too technical. The bottom line is this: The Holy Spirit cannot be pumped and scooped. He cannot be slung around, gathered up, or dispensed. He's not pixie dust. In this sense, there is no such thing as the Holy Spirit, because the Holy Spirit is not a *thing* at all, but the very presence of the personal God himself—with us, in us, and around us.

Yes, the Holy Spirit's power is something we really do experience, really do have access to, really can be more (or less) aware of—that is what this entire book is about, after all—but we never, in any sense whatsoever, can think of ourselves as controlling the Holy Spirit. You may as well try controlling ten thousand hurricanes at once. "The wind blows where it wishes, and you hear its sound, but you do not know where it comes from or where it goes. So it is with everyone who is born of the Spirit" (John 3:8).

So it is. This power, this real power straight from heaven, the power of the presence of God in our lives for all eternity, is not something you can step into and out of at your leisure. You can't do that any more than you can step into and out of your union with Christ. The presence of the power of the Holy Spirit is an ongoing reality for those who trust in Jesus, not because you perform but because he has promised.

The Powerful Spirit from Jesus

Put yourself in the shoes—or sandals—of Jesus' disciples for a moment. You've walked and talked with your Lord up close and personal for three years, and it has ended in a way you did not expect. It has ended, in fact, in crushing defeat. All along he was saying things about dying and "going away," but you always thought he was speaking metaphorically, like when he told one of those cryptic stories he was always telling. You didn't think he meant he was actually going to be delivered up and killed, much less that he was going to rise again on the third day. That's apocalyptic talk, nothing to be taken literally.

Then it turns out he wasn't just telling stories. He really was delivered up and killed. And you did nothing to stop it. If you've imagined yourself as Judas, or even Peter, you betrayed him. But none of the disciples gets away untarnished. You slept while he was praying in agony in the Garden. You ran away when he was arrested. You watched helplessly as he died, or more likely, kept your distance, lest the same fate befall you.

The disciples were a lot like us modern Christians in that they listened to Jesus' words constantly and yet still believed things he continually warned them not to believe and trusted in things he continually warned them not to trust. Even as Peter was chopping off the guard's ear, he was showing he didn't get it. He still thought the kingdom would come by violence. He was trusting in what his people had trusted in for centuries: human power.

So Jesus has been executed. And you're torn between grief and confusion and guilt. You miss your friend who knew you better than you knew yourself, who loved you freely and unconditionally, who served you even as he led you. You're confused because you saw him work all kinds of miraculous healings and wonders, and you assumed he was immortal, that surely he could have stopped his own murder. So why didn't he? And you feel guilt because you didn't do enough to stop it, didn't say enough to him while he was with you, didn't express your faith the best you could. If only you had another chance.

And then you do.

Try to imagine what it would be like to be overcome by grief and guilt and confusion, hopelessly and desperately so. The dream is over. And then imagine it suddenly, startlingly beginning again!

Jesus is back. And if you're Peter, you've already had a tearful encounter with this friend you've betrayed, this friend who died for you and now stands before you, the risen, glorified Lord of the universe, walking and talking and breathing again. And he's not mad at you. Can you imagine that?

Not only is he not mad at you, but he forgives you, restores you, and commissions you to keep on with the mission. How happy would you be? How excited would you be?

Then imagine he begins to say good-bye again. So soon after!

"Jesus, you just came back!"

"I know."

"We thought we lost you forever!"

"I know."

"We thought we were lost forever."

"I know."

"And now you're saying you're going away again?"

"Yes."

"Please don't do this to us!"

His leaving might seem cruel. You might feel hopeless all over again.

Or you might figure that this is really the end of the world. Maybe this is the time you finally arrive.

> So when they had come together, they asked him, "Lord, will you at this time restore the kingdom to Israel?" He said to them, "It is not for you to know times or seasons that the Father has fixed by his own authority. But you will receive power when the Holy Spirit has come upon you, and you will be my witnesses in Jerusalem and in all Judea and Samaria, and to the end of the earth." And when he had said these things, as they were looking on, he was lifted up, and a cloud took him out of their sight. (Acts 1:6–9)

God's grace truly is amazing. Here you, his disciples, come after the resurrection, still not getting it, still looking for some earthly power, some worldly consummation of the wonders you've beheld. And Jesus does not get angry. He simply continues in the promise he made before his death:

> Now I am going to him who sent me, and none of you asks me, "Where are you going?" But because I have said these things to you, sorrow has filled your heart. Nevertheless, I tell you the

truth: it is to your advantage that I go away, for if I do not go away, the Helper will not come to you. But if I go, I will send him to you (John 16:5–7).

He made this promise before his crucifixion, and he repeats it before his ascension. "When I'm gone, I'm not going to leave you alone, because the Holy Spirit is going to come and live with you forever."

This is the promise Jesus makes to all who will believe in the Son. It is not that we will be able to control some strange force, access some mystical power. No, he gives us the promise of the presence of the mighty God himself. "I am with you always," Jesus promises, "to the end of the age" (Matt. 28:20).

How can this be true if Jesus has ascended to heaven? How can this be true if we, like his disciples after his ascension, cannot look him in the eyes or hold his hand?

It is true because his Spirit is here with us—with *all* of us, not just twelve of us! And he is with all of us all over the world, not just the twelve of us in first-century Palestine. This is why pastor J. D. Greear said that "the Spirit inside you is better than Jesus beside you": "Unlike Jesus, our ministry is not restricted to only one geographical sector. When Jesus was on earth, his miraculous work was contained to wherever he was at the moment. Now that he is *in* us, his power is wherever we are. Thus, the extent of our works, which he does through us by the Spirit, is greater than anything he accomplished himself in his earthly incarnation."[5]

Despite this reasoning, Greear's words here may strike you as confusing or troubling. But he is drawing from the promise of Christ himself: "Truly, truly, I say to you, whoever believes in me will also do the works that I do; and greater works than

these will he do, because I am going to the Father" (John 14:12).
Greear is just taking Jesus at his own word.

Maybe you thought "greater works" referred to more spectacular miracles, or more of them. Maybe it takes you right back
to our opening question: Why don't we see the same kinds of
miracles today that we see in the Bible?

But don't you see that in fact we see better ones?

In another part of my life, I spent some time as a freelance
editor, and I remember working on a book manuscript for a rather
prominent pastor that centered on Jesus' promise in John 14:12.
The working title of that book, I am afraid to tell you, was *Better
Than Jesus*. According to John 14:12, this author contended, Jesus
promised we'd do better things than him, that we'd be *better* than
him. Unfortunately, I was only hired for my proofreading exper-
tise, not for my writing skills or theological insights, or I would
have changed a lot more in that manuscript than spelling and
punctuation!

This pastor had decided to resolve the confusion arising from
Jesus' promise in one way. I propose it may be resolved in a better
way. Suppose Jesus meant not that we'd be raising the dead more
than he did and walking on more water and healing more blind
people, but instead that he'd be more effective through his Spirit
indwelling billions of people around the world over multiple centuries than he would by incarnating among thousands in one
region in one lifetime?

The truth of the gospel may be spread more effectively this
way. The love of God may be felt more widely this way. And
getting back to the question of awesome miracles, isn't one soul
saved from eternal damnation better than a thousand lame men
walking again? Even Jesus makes this distinction: "Which is

easier, to say to the paralytic, 'Your sins are forgiven,' or to say, 'Rise, take up your bed and walk'?" (Mark 2:9).

Well? Which is the greater feat? A paralytic may get his legs back, but if he doesn't get his sins forgiven, he can enjoy those legs for the rest of his life, then spend the far longer time after his death in the fires of hell.

If you have the gift of eternal life, then no matter what else is going on in your life, you have the promise of mysterious power from God himself securing your soul from destruction. Why would you need another miracle?

The challenge now is walking every day in the power we've already been given.

CHAPTER 3

PRESSING "RESET" EVERY DAY

Experiencing the Spirit's Guidance

McDonald's golden arches may as well stand for "miracle," they hold such sway over children. When researchers from the Stanford University School of Medicine and the Johns Hopkins Bloomberg School of Public Health tested preschool-aged kids on their brand and logo recognition,[1] they discovered that, on this subject, most of these children were geniuses. Two- to six-year-olds could easily identify familiar brand names and packaging, and even if they did not know the name of the company, they could connect the logo with the product it was most known for.

Further, the researchers discovered that even if a hamburger, for instance, did not come from McDonald's, telling some kids that it did resulted in higher satisfaction with the taste than from the kids who knew they weren't eating a McDonald's burger. Not only did these kids know their logos, but they had bought the message of the logo advertising hook, line, and sinker. It changed their tastes!

Now, none of these kids had ever studied product marketing techniques. And their parents did not quiz them with company logo flash cards every night. They had not taken any classes on brand awareness. No, they knew their brands because kids these days are swimming in them. From billboards to book covers, television ads to (thanks to product placement) television shows, radio jingles to Internet pop-ups, product logos need no study; they are simply part of our environment. They *are* our environment. Advertising is the wallpaper of modern life.

The cumulative effect of routine exposure to company branding is just one aspect of the way we are all shaped by the daily messages of our consumer culture. The message is practically subliminal; none of us would assent, after all, to a letter in the mail that simply said, "Be more selfish." But that is the message we are hearing—and heeding—nonetheless. Sure, we may laugh at the idea that buying the world a Coca-Cola will teach it to live in perfect harmony, but plenty of us live as though the morning drive through Starbucks or the afternoon trip to the machine for a diet soda are what will keep our day on an even keel.

The truth is, the messages of the environments we are most in and the routines we most practice shape our attitudes and behaviors.

They do this in two ways: by bombarding us with their presence and by appealing to our appetites. We all know that using Apple computers won't really make us cool, but those Mac versus PC ads from a few years back succeeded like few other advertising campaigns have in identifying a desirable culture—hip, witty, smart—with Apple products. Consequently, Apple gains more market share with artists and other creative types while tech geeks still largely continue to swear by the "uncool" PC machines. Apple has succeeded in bombarding us with their advertising and appealing to our desire to identify with the "cool kids."

The Coca-Cola Company has succeeded in identifying their brand with America itself. Coke products and advertising are seen less as marketing and more as nostalgic vignettes of Americana. We may all laugh at what is truly implied in the slogan "Coke is it!" but Coca-Cola isn't the number-one soft drink in the world because everyone just said, "Nah."

If Christians are going to maintain a vibrant spiritual life in this culture where a soda (or some other product or experience) is "it," we must first understand how these ubiquitous messages form our values. Then we must learn how to subvert these messages with the one message that is the only source of actual power.

Think of our friend Bill, the fellow we met in chapter 1. During most of his week, as he lives the life of his Normal Self, he is exposed to countless messages—warnings, advice, promises—that are shaping his thinking and behavior, usually without him even knowing it. He might not be able to tell you why he has started feeling somewhat anxious and distant from the peace of God, but spending his morning absentmindedly consuming cable news certainly has something to do with that.

Many of you reading this book probably go about your lives in an environment much like Bill's. If you're "normal"—by the world's standards, anyway—you probably struggle to find time to be with friends. If you're married, statistically speaking, you probably don't interact much with your spouse in the morning. Either you've left for work before he or she is up or vice versa; or if you're both up, you're so preoccupied with preparing for the day (work, school, kids, whatever) that you don't have time. At the end of the day, one or both of you are too tired to engage on any substantive level. There's dinner, maybe kids to feed and bathe and put to bed, and then it's chill-out time with Netflix or a good book. If this describes you, even your daily access to family and coworkers may not compensate for a deep-seated sense of loneliness.

Then, whenever you emerge into the world or let the world into your home, the messages you receive are overwhelmingly directed at your individual self. Every word that comes from the world appears to appeal to your sense of self-sovereignty and your individual significance.

We daily face the temptation of self-worship. And we don't need any help with this! The inclination of our spirit is to place ourselves at the center of our universe, to "look out for number one." This is a constant struggle for anyone living anywhere, but the difficulty is exacerbated in a consumer culture that, in the savvy appeal of Burger King, wants us to "have it our way."

One of the sad ironies of Westernized living is how close together everyone is despite the stubborn maintaining of individualism. Our traffic is congested, our grocery stores are packed, our malls are busy, even our homes are sometimes eight feet away from each other on either side. Yet we are all doing our level best to mind our own business and see to it that everyone else minds theirs.

Our modern self-orientation holds out the promise of needlessness but ironically only enhances our sense of need. This is a modern tragedy that has effects on nearly all aspects of our lives, overflowing into every compartment of ourselves.

In the bestselling book *Bowling Alone*,[2] psychologist Robert

Putnam examines the detrimental effect of increased individualism and personal isolation even in congested urban and suburban areas. The title references that once-great American pastime: bowling. For so long a staple of suburban communal recreation, bowling leagues and parties have decreased. More and more people are bowling alone.

Putnam argues that this development is merely reflective of the larger decrease in what he calls "social capital," the amassed connections between individual people and community groups that contribute to the overall health of both individuals and communities.[3] We can see the "bowling alone" effect in our own neighborhoods. When I was a child—not that long ago!—the neighborhood streets and yards were noisy with children riding bikes, playing tag or football, and the like. Neighborhood children would play "army" in the woods or gather on curbs and sing songs.

These days many suburban neighborhoods are eerily quiet. All the children are inside, I suppose, playing video games or surfing the Internet. By themselves. Or they've been conscripted into the sacred liturgy of modern family life, zipping along from soccer practice to piano lessons to Scout meetings, and on and on, replicating in miniature the overscheduled routines of their parents.

To prove there is really nothing new under the sun (Eccl. 1:9), take a look at what Mark Twain wrote in the late 1860s about New York City: "It is a splendid desert—a domed and steepled solitude, where the stranger is lonely in the midst of a million of his race."[4] Is there a better spiritual summing up of the city—or the suburbs—than a place where millions of people can be alone together?

But city dwellers and suburbanites aren't the only ones keeping to themselves. During my time pastoring in rural Vermont, I became keenly aware of the "Yankee independence" typical of a vast many New Englanders. Rugged individualism, after all, is as American as apple pie. (Which we now buy in single servings from vending machines.)

The consumer culture most of us live in says this situation is fine and dandy. It accommodates our self-centeredness and affirms it, encouraging our natural inclination to think relationships and concern for others are overrated and unnecessary.

Suburbia is great at getting us onto a track. Like our friend Bill, we stay on our track daily, taking the same route: bed to car, car to work, work to car, car to garage. The track is predictable, comfortable. We know what to expect on our track. Our track doesn't ask much of us but to go with the flow. Our track, actually, is a rut. And while we keep our head down in this daily rut, people pass us on all sides, most of them in ruts of their own, and all of us living, as Thoreau said, "lives of quiet desperation."[5]

This is the rhythm of individualism, of self-reliance and self-sovereignty. It is seductive in its self-centeredness and destructive in its spiritual power.

When Jesus, and John the Baptist before him, began calling the world around them to attention, they preached, "Repent, for the kingdom of God is at hand!" Jesus wanted to get people *off* track. That's essentially what *repent* means: turn away from the way you're going and go a new way. That new way is the kingdom of God being brought to bear in the world by the power of the Holy Spirit.

In our day, as in Jesus' day, the track of the world is individualistic, consumeristic, self-centered, and self-concerned. Repentance, therefore, is an about-face from our way toward the self-crucifying way of God.

When Bill veered off his typical course, even just a little bit, he got different results. A small pang of dissatisfaction drove him to check out a Sunday school class, remember? And his short confession of aimlessness led to a classmate praying for him, however briefly. Taking a tiny break from his self-contained, self-conscious routine made a tiny difference in his outlook.

The next step for Bill, as for all of us, would be to consciously, intentionally, and more thoroughly get outside of his self-interested business as usual. For Bill and for us, this involves taking stock of our lives, being fearlessly honest about what our daily routines and our routine attitudes tell us about what we believe in, where we're finding satisfaction, and how we hope to live the life God has designed for us to live. We can't address a problem if we can't diagnose it. This process also involves becoming more and more aware of God's presence in our lives—in our entire lives, in every second and in every square inch, not simply during the moments we designate as "religious" or "spiritual." This is the point we decide not just to wait on a miracle, but to take the miracle we've already been given and wield it like a sledgehammer to the walls dividing our inner life and the worldly tracks guiding our outer trajectory.

We could call this "pressing the reset button" on our lives, going back to the beginning of our beliefs, assumptions, and ambitions and seeking to align them more closely with God's way. The Bible typically calls this "walking by the Spirit" (Gal. 5:16). Either way, what we're focusing on is *focusing*—intentionally creating more awareness in ourselves of the Spirit's work in our lives.

Putting Spiritual Awareness into Physical Practice

You probably know some people who seem in danger of thinking about the Holy Spirit too much. Of course, this isn't really possible if one is thinking rightly of the Holy Spirit. To think rightly of the Spirit is to think in a trinitarian fashion—meaning, we think of the Spirit in relation to the first and second persons of the Godhead and how each works distinctly and together to save us and help us "work out" our salvation.

But you know people are off track when they talk a lot about the Spirit to the neglect of Jesus and his revealed Word. Sometimes these people long for a word from the Spirit so much that they become dissatisfied with the Bible, which is itself a word from the Holy Spirit who inspired it and which tells us everything we need to be completely equipped for every good work (2 Tim. 3:16–17). And when you spend time with these people or in these people's kinds of churches, you often hear more about the Spirit than you do the Son. They believe giving more attention to the Spirit strikes a kind of balance, especially since there are people who don't think of the Spirit at all. But those who practice this kind of spiritual thinking are way off track, since the Holy Spirit's purpose is to point our attention continually to Jesus. (It's for this reason that some theologians have sometimes referred to the Holy Spirit as the "shy" member of the Trinity; his role among us is largely to glorify the Son.[6])

Let's be honest: sometimes the people who seem to talk a lot about the Holy Spirit just seem downright kooky. And they are just as much in error as those who think of the Spirit too little. Ironically, both of these extremes are exercises, really, in self-worship. This is especially true for all those in our modern age who equate the Spirit's presence with health, wealth, and other circumstantial blessings. The Holy Spirit-obsessed constantly run the risk of the error explored in chapter 2—thinking of *him* as an *it*. Things are going well, and "the Spirit-filled life" sounds a lot like "May the force be with you."

But this is not consistent with actual Spirit-led Christianity, as C. S. Lewis aptly showed:

> When you are feeling fit and the sun is shining and you do not want to believe that the whole universe is a mere mechanical dance of atoms, it is nice to be able to think of this great mysterious Force rolling on through the centuries and carrying you on its crest. If, on the other hand, you want to do something shabby, the Life-Force, being only a blind force, with no morals and no mind, will never interfere with you like that troublesome God we learned about when we were children. The Life-Force is a sort of tame God. You can switch it on when you want, but it will not bother you. All the thrills of religion and none of the cost.[7]

But the real Holy Spirit who is God is always blessedly meddling. And it's exactly the cost Lewis talks about here that the real Holy Spirit means to help us with. Thus, "walking by the Spirit" must entail fixation on Christ.

If we are thinking rightly of the Spirit, it's impossible to think too much of him, because he is constantly pointing us to the Son of God, unto whom we are to take every thought captive (2 Cor. 10:5).

As we saw with the Stanford fast-food logo study, we don't

have to practice awareness of corporate branding to become experts. Simply by being immersed in this world, we become experts by a kind of cultural osmosis. Our friend Bill, likewise, could not discern how his daily routine was set up precisely to frustrate his sense of direction and fulfillment. He was awash in messages that thwarted him, despite the fact that he never focused on any of them. You don't have to be using your mind very much to have your mind shaped by what you're consuming.

But the Holy Spirit was working in Bill all along. And the Holy Spirit was speaking all along, too, using Bill's own mindless decisions and reflexive practices to chip away at his numb satisfaction. It's a bit like breathing, actually. It keeps you alive! But I bet you hardly ever think about your breathing until it is somehow compromised—you get out of breath exercising or short of breath at a high altitude or get the wind knocked out of you falling down. Most other times we don't have to be conscious of our breathing, and yet we still breathe. We can even be unconscious and yet still breathe.

The Holy Spirit is sort of like that. (Incidentally, both the Hebrew and Greek words for "spirit"—*ruach* and *pneuma*, respectively—are also synonymous with "breath" and "air," or "wind.") Regardless of whether you're conscious of the Spirit's work in your life, he is still working. He doesn't need you to help him. He is who he is and he does what he does.

Just as with our breathing, though, we don't often think about the Holy Spirit until something goes wrong. And just as with our breathing, thinking more consciously about the Holy Spirit, even in times of comfort, can be hugely beneficial.

Fitness experts will tell you that breathing exercises are extremely helpful as you are working out. Some will tell you to breathe in through your nose and out through your mouth. One fitness coach I had used to remind me to breathe when I was doing abdominal exercises. My default response was to hold my breath, not for any intentional reason. But he reminded me that concentrating on my breathing would help with my energy and endurance both in the moment and in the long run. Concentrating on respiration helps runners develop stamina, divers and swimmers increase depth and speed, and other athletes in general oxygenate their muscles and stay more mentally alert.

I'm not trying to oversell this. I'm not really talking about breathing at all. I'm talking about how practicing awareness of the Spirit's breath in your own spirit can enhance your sense of peace with God and increase your affections for him.

After getting home from church that Sunday, having experienced a bit of the Spirit's help through prayer and fellowship, Bill determined to stop taking the Holy Spirit for granted. He resolved to press "reset" on his daily life and to practice more awareness of God's presence.

So how could he do that?

Life-Hacking Your Spiritual Awareness

Taking time to consider a reset of our daily life is a good exercise for us all. It's important to take stock of our surroundings, our routines, our assumptions and attitudes, comparing everything to the kind of life Jesus has called us into to see if anything is lacking. Below I suggest a few diagnostic questions to help you determine how off track you may be from the Spirit-aware life and how much of a reset you will need.

- Do you constantly or often feel hurried, even when you don't need to be?
- Do you waste a lot of time watching TV or browsing social media?
- Do the status updates or images from your happy friends online stress you out, irritate you, depress you, or tempt you with jealousy?
- If a neighbor or family member buys something new, do you begin thinking about how to acquire the same product?
- Do you feel trapped in regular cycles of dysfunction or conflict with people close to you?
- Do you feel "stuck" in your relationship with your spouse or children or siblings or parents, in some kind of relational impasse you lack the energy or wisdom to handle?
- Do you struggle with regular church attendance?
- Do you struggle with feeling connected when you do attend church?
- Are you too busy in the morning and too exhausted in the evening to spend any focused time reading your Bible?
- Do you pray only in moments of crisis, as a kind of "last resort"?

If you answered yes to more than one of those questions, it is very likely you are suffering from a severe deprivation of Spiritual awareness. Each of those diagnostic questions reveals a symptom of the essential problem we all face of going about our lives in our own wisdom and in our own power. And as perhaps you're beginning to see, this is not the kind of wisdom or power that gives us the kind of life we really want. Nor is it the kind of life God wants us to live.

Even if you could get everything you wanted—financially, relationally, physically, and emotionally—but you had it all with very little thought of God and the experience of his power, your life, as comfortable as it might seem, would be an unmitigated disaster. Because the worst thing that can happen to you is to get everything you want and be extremely comfortable for a long time yet be relationally disconnected from God. Separation from God is tragic, and it is tragic how few people feel that separation.

So it is a severe mercy when the Spirit puts that rock in our shoe, when he gives us those little irritating nudges or gnawing pangs that help us to realize we're missing out on the most important part of life—knowing God, which is of course not really a *part* of life, but life itself!

Bill is listening. And as he heads into that boardroom of his interior life to fire all the compartment directors who challenge Jesus for supremacy, he begins making some changes in his life to help him redirect his thoughts and vision. He wants to practice more awareness of the Spirit's presence in his life and the Spirit's guidance into the life of Christ. He thinks through some "life hacks" for his daily routines. Maybe you can incorporate some of these as well:

- Bill puts his Bible underneath his phone on his nightstand when he goes to bed, so when he wakes up in the morning with the alarm, its presence at his hand triggers him to spend a little time reading it.
- He sets himself a time limit at first—fifteen minutes—so that it feels more manageable and he doesn't get

overwhelmed. As the discipline becomes more routine, he increases his timer to twenty minutes and eventually thirty. To compensate for this time in his morning prework schedule, he sets his alarm to wake him five minutes earlier, then ten minutes.

- Bill subscribes to a daily devotional that sends him an e-mail so that he has a regular reminder in his inbox to spend some time in God's Word.

- Instead of mindlessly listening to music or business podcasts on his commute, Bill subscribes to some sermon podcasts recommended by friends and listens to preaching on the drive.

- As Bill becomes more involved at his church, he begins keeping track of prayer requests in his class and keeps this notebook in his car so he's always reminded to pray for them.

- Bill discovers that his church maintains a membership directory, so he gets a copy and puts it in his Bible as a reminder to pray for a few of his fellow churchgoers during his devotional time.

- Bill discovers that reading in bed at night instead of watching TV or surfing the Internet is not just a more useful way to spend that time, it's more restful.

One thing you will notice that Bill has done is minimize the amount of time he exposes himself to consumeristic and materialistic messages—whether from TV, radio, or the web. This is not because enjoying certain forms of entertainment is bad. It's not because movies or social media are sinful. It's only because Bill has come to realize his hunger for more of what God might be saying to him, and he has become suspicious of how the thoughtless exposure to other messages might be shaping his mind and heart without him realizing it.

Over time what Bill discovers is that he begins to feel more rested, more alert, and more content. He begins to invent more life hacks to keep himself aware of God's presence. These new practices and routines don't ward off pain or trouble, but they do prepare him for dealing with difficulty in more Spirit-attuned ways.

The other thing you will notice is how many of Bill's life hacks have to do with taking in the Bible. This is not incidental. Bill is not interested in becoming more religious. He has tried this before and realizes it doesn't work. What he does begin to suspect, however, is that the difficulty he has had with taking in the Bible is due to how different its message sounds and how differently it works. We'll discuss that more in chapter 4. Bill is trusting that his short, daily time in the Bible will provide a payoff further down the road. Like the weight lifter just starting out, he knows he's not going to be benching four hundred pounds on day one.

What Bill doesn't understand is that even when he isn't "feeling it," the Spirit is using God's Word to empower him in the very moment of his reading.

How the Christian Life Works

Do you remember the film *The Karate Kid*? The original one with the ageless wonder Ralph Macchio? Back in the eighties, every movie it seemed had a training montage of some kind.

The archetypal training montage was established by *Rocky* and its sequels. But almost every other movie after that had a preparation scene of some sort—for an athletic contest, a party, a test, a battle, even (twice that I can think of) a boat race!—set to an inspirational song. Well, in *The Karate Kid*, as you'll recall, the training montage was spread out over many scenes, and they played out very deceptively. The hero of the film, Daniel, is commanded by his sensei, Mr. Miyagi, to wash and wax his entire lot of used cars. A little confused, Daniel nevertheless complies. He spends hours washing and waxing. "Wax on. Wax off." Remember?

Eventually, Daniel isn't just waxing cars; he's also painting Mr. Miyagi's fence ("Up, down") and house ("Side to side") and even sanding his extensive backyard deck ("Sand the floor"). By the end of all these chores, Daniel is tired, frustrated, sore, and wondering when he's actually going to learn karate.

Fed up with the routine and rigorous labor, Daniel says he's going to quit—until Mr. Miyagi asks him to repeat the motions of each task. Wax on, wax off. Up, down. Side to side. Sand the floor. Then Miyagi begins sparring with him, and Daniel is astounded to discover that his daily labor has built into his physical system the reflexes needed to defend himself from attack.[8] It's a really great scene, and the disciplines of the Christian life are a lot like that.

At first, and perhaps for a while, we may be wondering if we're getting anywhere. Reading the Bible can be slow going, sometimes frustrating or confusing. I just finished reading Leviticus in my Bible-reading schedule, and it doesn't matter how many times I read Leviticus (admittedly not many times, but a few!)—I still find much of it sluggish and repetitive. I wonder, *Do I really need to know this stuff?*

Of course, some parts of the Bible are easier to read and apply than others. But like our friend Bill, we discover that if we put a little time and effort in, daily encounters with God's Word are shaping us and training us in ways we don't quite see until we really need to see.

In Luke 12 Jesus warned his disciples about coming persecution. He told them that they would be brought for questioning before rulers and authorities. But he said to them, "Do not be anxious about how you should defend yourself or what you should say, for the Holy Spirit will teach you in that very hour what you ought to say" (12:11–12). I don't know that Jesus was telling them that the Holy Spirit would miraculously give them answers in the moment, like somebody helping you cheat on a test might give you the answers through a hidden earpiece. I think Jesus was telling them that the Holy Spirit would miraculously give them the answers, bringing to their minds in their moment of need the things Jesus himself had been teaching and would be continuing to teach them.

When we press "reset" on our lives, declaring "message bankruptcy" in order to start over with incremental exposure to God's Word, we are preparing ourselves to be led by God's Spirit in new, fresh, and ever-real ways. The result of this commitment to training is that our instincts and impulses are rewired, our thoughts and attitudes are renewed, and our words and actions are reconnected to the empowering presence of Christ in us. We end up doing, as Sinclair Ferguson wrote, "the 'natural' thing spiritually and the 'spiritual' thing naturally."[9]

This is how the Christian life is designed to work: from beginning to end, the Holy Spirit envelops us in the loving will of God, seeding promise after promise in us and sending power after power through us by his breathed-out, infallible Word. In fact, we cannot even live apart from the Word of God.

It's good news, then, that God has not left us to figure things out on our own. He has spoken and he continues to speak. It's important, however, that we learn how to listen to his voice.

CHAPTER 4

ENGAGING THE DIVINE DIALOGUE

Experiencing the Spirit's Voice

Have you ever felt like God was holding out on you?

I remember a particularly excruciating time in my life when nothing was going right. Everything I loved seemed cold toward me; everything that gave me joy was gone; everything I believed God had called me to do was out of reach. A dark cloud of depression settled over me, and for a while I even battled suicidal thoughts.

Oddly enough, in the midst of that emotional and spiritual pain, I never doubted that God existed. But I *did* feel like he didn't care about me. I would pray deep, desperate prayers, and they seemed to echo against a vast brick wall where the throne of God used to be. I thought God was shutting me out.

In his now-classic novel *Silence*, Shūsaku Endō presents one of the most masterful explorations in the history of literature of this painful experience. The story follows some of the first

Christian missionaries to Japan, where the Christian faith had been outlawed and adherents were being meticulously persecuted. Against the bloody backdrop of interrogation and torture, Father Rodrigues wrestles constantly with God's apparent apathy toward the plight of the suffering faithful. "Already twenty years have passed since the persecution broke out; the black soil of Japan has been filled with the lament of so many Christians; the red blood of priests has flowed profusely; the walls of churches have fallen down; and in the face of this terrible and merciless sacrifice offered up to Him, God has remained silent."[1]

What seems especially hard to fathom is how God could give the cold shoulder to people who were giving their very lives for him. In one particularly haunting passage, the mournful ambiance of a merciless creation is compared with the infinite echo chamber of the divine, as if the only response to the suffering of God's children is a kind of undisturbed "white noise":

> The sound of those waves that echoed in the dark like a muffled drum; the sound of those waves all night long as they broke meaninglessly, receded, and then broke again on the shore. This was the sea that relentlessly washed the dead bodies of Mokichi and Ichizo, the sea that swallowed them up, the sea that, after their death, stretched out endlessly with unchanging expressions. And like the sea God was silent. His silence continued.[2]

Rodrigues feels abandoned by his heavenly Father. The conversation feels one-sided. In Martin Scorsese's film adaptation, Rodrigues whispers into the air, "I pray but I am lost. Am I just praying to silence?"

Have you ever been there?

So many times, especially in times of difficulty, a relationship with God can feel hard to come by. Every motivational slogan, every inspirational meme reminding us of God's will for our lives can seem more and more cliché. Why? Because God doesn't speak in the ways we most often desire. He doesn't speak in the ways that are easiest to hear. And in times of hardship and pain, it often feels like he doesn't speak at all.

Even the most devout among us have endured this feeling. It sometimes lasts a very long time. For some it never seems to go away. After Mother Teresa passed away, many people were shocked to learn from her journals and personal letters that she battled feeling unheard (and unloved) by God for a long, long time. In a letter to one confidant, she wrote, "Jesus has a very special love for you. As for me, the silence and emptiness is so great that I look and do not see, listen and do not hear."[3]

What do you do when you feel like God isn't speaking to you?

We must remember in these painful moments (and seasons) of life that our relationship with God isn't identical to our relationships with other people. There's the issue of visibility, of course. Even friends you don't live close to can be seen online or heard on the phone. You can dialogue with them instantaneously. Relationship with God is less instant, less tangible. And yet the Bible still speaks of our relationship with God in terms of realness, intimacy, and depth.

God isn't just sending messages. In fact, he is making friends.

"No longer do I call you servants," Jesus said to his disciples; "I have called you friends" (John 15:15). The sweetness of this declaration belies its staggering import. Jesus Christ is the holy and anointed King of the universe. He upholds the universe. He is the ferocious Lion of Judah and the spotless Lamb of God. He is the Alpha and the Omega, the first and the last, the beginning and the end. He is the Lord of lords, the great I AM in the flesh, God incarnate. And yet he called these ruffians and rednecks *friends.*

They are not worthy to untie his sandals. But he embraces them.

I think of Exodus 33:11, which tells us that God used to speak to Moses "face to face, as a man speaks to his friend." I don't rightly know what this entailed. What does it look like to speak face-to-face with God? I imagine it might have involved a *Christophany*—a preincarnate manifestation of the Son of God who could relate with Moses visibly, audibly, tangibly. We have other examples of such theophanies (visible appearances of God) throughout the Old Testament, but Exodus 33:11 is one of my favorites because it displays the glory of the Lord Most High in an intimate, brotherly way. God isn't wrestling with Moses as with Jacob or spiritually disintegrating him as with Isaiah. He is chatting with Moses, like you and I might chat at a cozy table in a breakfast nook. This scene makes me think of Moses having coffee with God.

Don't you long for such an experience? I do.

The truth is, these words apply to everyone who has been justified by faith in Jesus Christ. Drawing from Genesis 15:6, James wrote, "The Scripture was fulfilled that says, 'Abraham believed God, and it was counted to him as righteousness'—and he was called a friend of God. You see that a person is justified by works and not by faith alone" (2:23–24). In this passage, James made theology strikingly personal. According to James, upright standing before God (justification) is inextricably connected to upright walking *with* God. This means that the gospel of Jesus

Christ, when believed, doesn't just make us square with God—it makes us friends with God.

I confess that words like these thrill my heart like almost no others. Given the sinfulness of my heart and the sheer number of my weaknesses and deficiencies, it is astounding to me that the Holy One of Israel would consider me a friend. Like the prodigal son in that pigsty (Luke 15:17–19), I figure that if there's any way back into my Father's good graces, it has to be through becoming a servant. But like the prodigal's father, our heavenly Father is welcoming us home as ones who *belong.*

Jesus says to all who have denied themselves and come after him: "Remember, you aren't my servants. You are my friends."

And what kind of friends never talk to each other?

The Divine Dialogue

First, let's do justice to the feeling of silence. If you have ever felt like God is holding out on you—or even feel that way right now—you are not alone! For Christians serious about their faith, this feeling can be rather commonplace, if only because they are so eager to hear from God. Superficial Christians and unbelievers rarely worry about whether God is giving them the silent treatment, since they aren't normally very interested in God's voice in the first place. They barely notice if they haven't received a word from God (and often barely notice when they do).

Even the "heroes" of the faith in the Bible struggled with a sense of God's silence. "Be not silent, O God of my praise!" David cried out (Ps. 109:1), as if his praise were in danger of landing against that brick wall. He wanted to be in dialogue with his Creator.

The same holds true for the sufferer of sufferers, Job. The long book that chronicles Job's journey from comfort through pain of all kinds (physical, emotional, spiritual) to satisfaction with the sovereignty of God contains perhaps the most extensive dialogue between a man and his Maker in all the Scriptures, and yet Job explained in his anguish, "I cry to you for help and you do not answer me; I stand, and you only look at me" (30:20). Job believed God could speak, or he wouldn't have cried out to him. And yet for Job, his circumstances seem louder. His pain was drowning out God's presence in his life. Or so he thought.

But we never see God going silent on his children in the Bible. Now, he may not have spoken the way they wanted or expected him to, but he didn't stop speaking, not really.

The experience of feeling God's silence is real, but the emphasis here should really be on the feeling. Because the truth is, God is never silent. When we take him to be silent, the problem is on our end. Francis Schaeffer explained the disrupted dynamic this way: "Because man revolted against God and tried to stand autonomous, the great alienation is in the area of man's separation from God. When that happened, then everything else went."[4]

In other words, sin cuts the telephone wires. This is part of God's judgment on sin, but the responsibility still falls on us. If we don't hear God, it is not because God is not speaking, but because we have gone deaf. "The heavens declare the glory of God, and the sky above proclaims his handiwork. Day to day pours out speech" (Ps. 19:1–2). Theologians call this general revelation. From the vast beauty of the sky and outer space to the dark mysteries of the Mariana Trench and secret wonders of hidden jungle caves, all creation is rehearsing the reality of God every day. God's own creation is announcing his presence. Even if you never picked up a Bible, you couldn't rightly say that God wasn't speaking, at least in some way.

Paul picked up this argument in Romans 1, where he said that man's failure to hear God is entirely man's fault, since creation itself has revealed his invisible attributes (vv. 18–20). The reason we don't hear God, whether generally in creation or specially in his written Word, is because our self-centered autonomy has disconnected us. This is how Schaeffer went on to explain it: "This autonomy is carried over into the very basic area of epistemology, of knowing, so that man is not only divided from other men in the area of knowing, he is divided from himself."[5]

Divided from himself? Doesn't this sound a bit like the compartmentalized life we spent some time deconstructing in chapters 1 and 2? It is this very approach to the Christian life that causes us so many problems when it comes to knowing God's will. We compartmentalize our feelings and experiences—connecting only good ones to God and never bad ones—and then wonder why we struggle to hear from him. The inability to see difficulties of all kinds, including suffering, as themselves being sent by God is a result of poor theology. It is evidence, in fact, of a poor doctrine of the Holy Spirit.

Perhaps the primary reason that in times of difficulty or loneliness we think of God as being silent is because we equate "God's voice" with material blessings, physical comfort, and happy feelings. When good things are happening, we are rarely troubled by God's silence, even if we never talk to him ourselves or read his Word.

The idea that blessings equate to God speaking while hardships equate to God's silence is a symptom of the way we tend to think of blessings as "normal" and hardship as "odd." Given the fallenness of humanity and the consequential brokenness of creation, this viewpoint is exactly upside down. We'll come back to the important question of what God the Spirit may be doing in the midst of our suffering in chapter 7, but for now, it is enough to say this: God is never really silent with us, not even in our loneliest and darkest circumstances. Hearing him may indeed be more difficult, and we may find "feeling" his presence harder still—that is only natural. Nonetheless, he is always with us and he is always speaking. Engaging in this heavenly conversation is the essence of walking by faith, not by sight. (I'll say a bit more on that in a minute.) The key to the supernatural life, then, is engaging in this divine dialogue for which all Christians are empowered to participate.

What is the divine dialogue? Put very simply, it works like this: God speaks to us in his Word, and we respond to him in prayer. God may speak to us in other ways, and we to him, but these are subjective and not normative. No, there is no other way around this truth: the primary way any Christian will participate in a friendship with God is by Bible study and prayer. Over this chapter and the next, we'll examine each of these components of the divine dialogue in turn.

God Is Not Silent

I have a friend whose road to Christian conversion began when he read a strange book on spiritual enlightenment by American

New Age mystic Ram Dass. The book, still an Amazon bestseller in the category of spiritualism, is titled *Be Here Now*, and it incorporates principles of yoga and other meditation techniques aimed at awakening readers to a new mode of existence, creating a high without the use of pharmaceuticals. For my friend, who came of age during the heyday of the '60s and who was beginning to get burnt out on the drug scene, the "free love" scene, and all the rest of the hippie movement, the promise of enlightenment was tantalizing. He found in *Be Here Now* a heady mix of Far East teaching, Buddhist proverbs, and all sorts of other religious ephemera, but Ram Dass had made one fatal mistake. He'd thrown thoughts and sayings from all sorts of spiritual traditions into his pseudospiritual literary gumbo—because of the idea that all religions contain elements of truth—but he had also included some Bible verses.

My friend said those verses seemed to jump off the page. The Bible passages seemed different from everything else around them. Thousands of seekers have read the heresy in *Be Here Now* and not noticed any difference among the religious quotations. But for at least one, the Bible in the book had an effect unintended by Ram Dass but wholly intended by the Spirit of God. Truly the Bible is "living and active" (Heb. 4:12).

The Bible is no ordinary book. And when Christians say that, they don't simply mean that it's a religious book or an otherwise special book compared to other books. We mean that the Bible is a supernatural book. It is a capital *S* Spiritual book because the words contained in it were breathed out by the Holy Spirit (2 Tim. 3:16).

We have, most of us, at our fingertips the very words from the mouth of God. And yet far too many of us live our Christian lives as if to say to this startling reality, "Eh. What else you got?"

We adopt this attitude every time we make short shrift of the power of Scripture and stake our hopes on some other power, some other sign from God. Do you remember the story Jesus told about the rich man and Lazarus? At the end of Luke 16, Jesus shares this parable, ostensibly about the afterlife. Lazarus is a poor man who dies and is then carried by angels to heaven. The rich man dies and winds up paying for his self-centered ways in the torments of Hades. Somehow the rich man is able to see Lazarus across the great cosmic divide, resting in comfort at Abraham's side. What is a rich man to do?

He acts like he has learned no lesson from his lifetime of self-worship. He asks Abraham to send Lazarus with relief, as if even in the afterlife the poor exist only to wait on the rich! But Abraham refuses the request because the divide between heaven and hell cannot be bridged in the world to come. The exchange that ensues is quite revealing, not just about the afterlife, but about the nature of signs and wonders:

> "I beg you, father, to send him to my father's house—for I have five brothers—so that he may warn them, lest they also come into this place of torment." But Abraham said, "They have Moses and the Prophets; let them hear them." And he said, "No, father Abraham, but if someone goes to them from the dead, they will repent." He said to him, "If they do not hear Moses and the Prophets, neither will they be convinced if someone should rise from the dead." (Luke 16:27–31)

The rich man has asked for a miraculous sign. A resurrection! This, he reasons, will ensure saving belief in God. Many people today think the same way. "I'd believe," they say, "if I could just see a sign." Even Christians sometimes think this way, arguing subconsciously with God, pleading for some kind of miracle to bolster their faith.

Remember, you don't need a miracle.

The Lord has spoken. And this is exactly what Abraham tells the rich man. If you don't believe the Word of God—"Moses and the Prophets"—no miracle will be any help to you.

The theological concept behind this important truth is called the "sufficiency of Scripture." Sufficiency of Scripture basically means that the Bible is all we need for all we need! Or, as Paul put it, the inspired words of God are more than enough to make the Christian "complete" and "equipped for every good work" (2 Tim. 3:17). We may receive more than God's Word, but it will never be better than God's Word or because God's Word is somehow lacking.

The gift of the Scriptures is the enduring presence of God's voice. As long as we have this book, he is never silent.

I think back to *Silence*'s Father Rodrigues watching his flock systematically murdered from his own prison, both literal and spiritual. He seems plagued more painfully by God's apparent silence over his ordeal than he is by the ordeal itself. *Why won't God say something?* he wonders. I confess that as I read the novel and even watched the movie, I couldn't help but see this central dilemma through the lens of my own reformed theology. As a good *sola scriptura* Protestant, I am compelled to mention that God *has* said something, that he is still saying something, and that he does say something about all that Rodrigues and the persecuted faithful are going through—he says it all through his written Word.

For instance, Jesus tells his followers that when they are

subjected to persecution for their faith, the Holy Spirit will help them in those very moments:

> When they bring you before the synagogues and the rulers and the authorities, do not be anxious about how you should defend yourself or what you should say, for the Holy Spirit will teach you in that very hour what you ought to say (Luke 12:11–12).

The apostle Paul spoke to the reality of martyrdom in Romans 8:35–37, but he offered up the superior reality of the prevailing love of God: "Who shall separate us from the love of Christ? Shall tribulation, or distress, or persecution, or famine, or nakedness, or danger, or sword? As it is written, 'For your sake we are being killed all the day long; we are regarded as sheep to be slaughtered.' No, in all these things we are more than conquerors through him who loved us."

Many more biblical texts instruct Christians undergoing persecution, prepare them for it, and encourage them through it. The reality is that God is neither blind to our suffering nor ambivalent about it.

Appropriate or not, I wondered throughout *Silence*'s depictions of this wrestling with the silence of God how a good evangelical understanding of special revelation might have been a comfort. There is little evidence that Rodrigues's familiarity with Scripture helps him sort out his theodicy (the tension of reconciling the idea of a good God with the existence of an evil world), apart from the obvious recollections of the betrayals of Judas and—to a much lesser extent—of Peter.

Rodrigues keeps looking for visions, listening for voices. He wants to see Jesus' face in the reflection of the water, hear Jesus' instructions wafting in on the wind. Meanwhile, as the grass is withering and the flower is fading, the Word of our God stands forever (Isa. 40:8).

This is why many churches conclude public Scripture readings with the declaration, "This is the Word of the Lord." It may seem to some like merely a liturgical flourish, some kind of rote religious formality. But for many of us, it is a way to remind our hearers and ourselves that these words are different, that these words are special, supernatural. These words come from God himself, and when they are read, whether silently or aloud, God is speaking.

No, God is not silent. Even when we feel like he is, he isn't. We may struggle to hear his voice, but very often that is because the dust is so thick on our copies of his Word.

And yet even when we are reading the Bible, we may be tempted to think something like, *It isn't working.*

Daily Dwelling in His Power

Our old friend Bill has been riding that Spiritual energy for several weeks after that "incident" at church. One of the ways it has affected him is in his commitment to daily Scripture reading. Bill previously understood that having a daily devotional time was important, and he'd given it the ol' college try multiple times throughout his young adult life. Every January 1, for instance, he'd make a resolution to work through one particular Bible reading plan or another. But always about late February or March, when the rigors of Leviticus were testing his attention span, monotony would set in and he'd drift away from interest in God's Word.

But lately he's tasted something new of the Spirit's work. He's come to believe that if God is speaking in one way through the shared communion of Spiritual fellowship in his church, surely he could be speaking in a better and clearer way through words that are Spiritually inspired.

Bill's perspective on the Bible is beginning to change. His disillusionment with his daily life—and the fading of all the shiny messages it presented to him every day—has primed his soul for the deeper frequency of God's infallible Word. This time, instead of beginning with a particular Bible reading plan, he simply picked a book—the gospel of Matthew—and began reading.

Without feeling the burden of checking something off his list, he discovers that he reads more slowly, more deliberately, simply trying to think about what he is reading. Some days he covers a lot of ground, while other days he simply reads a few verses. But the consistency of daily reading begins to take hold, mainly because Bill is approaching the Bible not as a religious token of routine affection but as Spiritual food to feed his hunger.

Bill finds Matthew's account of the temptation of Jesus particularly helpful in processing his own spiritual journey.

You likely recall that before Jesus began his earthly teaching ministry, the Holy Spirit led him out into the wilderness to be tempted by the Devil. That knowledge alone should help us broaden our horizon about the kinds of things the Spirit does in our lives. Despite what the prosperity gospelists say, it is not the more spiritual person who has everything going his way. Sometimes the Spirit leads us right into the valley of the shadow of death so that we might learn to rely more fully on God for our satisfaction and sustenance.

Our Lord Jesus himself faced this painful dilemma and all the temptations that came with it. Tired, alone, and famished in the wilderness, he encountered the Devil, who urged him to turn stones to bread. Jesus replied by quoting Deuteronomy 8:3: "Man shall not live by bread alone, but by every word that comes from the mouth of God" (Matt. 4:4).

In fact, all three times Jesus replied to the Devil's temptation, he quoted a Bible verse. For every point of accusation and allurement, Jesus responded with, "As it is written. . . ."

Even Jesus affirmed *sola scriptura*.

This approach to spiritual survival in the wilderness of life is especially notable given the historic temptation that Jesus was redeeming. The Bible calls Jesus "the last Adam" (1 Cor. 15:45), having the final and redemptive word over the colossal spiritual collapse of the first Adam. If you remember, way back in the early pages of Genesis, the fall of humankind began with a very similar temptation. Adam and Eve were in the garden, and the serpent came to Eve with three baited hooks, just as he later approached Jesus: the forbidden fruit looked good to the eyes, it looked good for the stomach, and it promised good for the consciousness. Satan even began by undermining Eve's sense of God's authoritative words. He said, "Did God really say . . . ?"

At first Eve was able to correct the misunderstanding: "No, actually, God said *this*, not that." But she eventually succumbed. Why? Essentially, she ran out of "thus saith the Lord." She wavered on her commitment to the sufficiency of God's Word. Eve ran out of Bible verses.

You and I must avoid this grave mistake at all costs. We are grateful that Christ's sinless enduring of temptation is part of his righteousness counted to our account, so that those of us who trust in him will never fall away, but we should also see Christ's enduring of temptation as an example to us. This is what J. I. Packer said:

> It is impossible to give too much weight to the fact that Jesus, who was himself God speaking, would have consistently viewed the words of his Bible as God speaking, and should have lived his life and fulfilled his vocation of teaching and suffering in direct and conscious obedience to what was written. Now, in effect, from his throne, he tells all who would be his disciples that they must learn from him and follow his example at this point and submit to becoming disciples of the canonical Scriptures. His authority and its for us are one.[6]

In other words, if Jesus' Bible was good enough for him, why isn't ours good enough for us? And further, what Packer is saying is that if we truly want to follow Jesus, we will take the Bible's words as if they are his. Because they are.

But Jesus' treatment of Scripture isn't just about how authoritative and sufficient it is, but also about how satisfying and sustaining it is. When times of loneliness, suffering, and even spiritual hunger overtake us, we must remember that it's not bread that keeps us alive, not really—it's the Word of God.

And not running out of Bible verses in the leanest circumstances of our lives means actively preparing for those moments by storing them up while we can.

The Holy Spirit has inspired this extraordinary book we call the Bible. "For no prophecy was ever produced by the will of man," the apostle Peter said, "but men spoke from God as they were carried along by the Holy Spirit" (2 Peter 1:21). And the

Holy Spirit is still using those words to carry people along. This is what happened to my hippie friend just trying to mind his own mystical business with *Be Here Now*. The Spirit of God spoke supernaturally to him, lifting his Word off those natural pages and carrying my friend along, up out of the licentiousness of the counterculture and onto the narrow path of Christ.

But the Holy Spirit speaks supernaturally through the words of the Bible even when we aren't "feeling it." When I lived in Vermont, I often enjoyed retreating to my backyard and relaxing by my fire pit. It gets really cold in Vermont. But often even the bitter cold wouldn't keep me away from my fire pit. Sometimes I would have to dig it out of the snow, but I'd throw some dry logs in there and light it up and cozy up close. The more the air around us grows cold, the harder it is to feel the warmth of the fire, but the warmth is still there. It's doing *something*.

The Bible is like that.

The Word of God isn't magic any more than prayer is. It's not a talisman. In Matthew 7 Jesus said that when the wise man builds his house on the rock, it's like building his life on the words of Christ himself. Notice that doing so doesn't ward off the storms. It simply ensures that your life won't be destroyed by them.

Day by day in the Bible, word by word, we are shoring up the foundation of our lives. The Spirit is actually doing this, planting these words deep in our hearts. We are warming ourselves by God's Spiritual fire when we stay close to his Word. You may not feel it, especially if circumstances in your life have led you into cold territory, but the Spirit is always at work, always breathing out, always stoking those flames, however meager. "A faintly burning wick he will not quench" (Isa. 42:3).

If you want to hear from God, you won't find his special

word for you out there in the ether, mysteriously coded in some mercurial "signs," or disguised in your self-interested intuition—you'll find it in those plain words typeset on the page, flickering on the screen, resounding from your church's stage or pulpit.

You don't need a miracle. You have one: a book straight from heaven.

And if we really believed that the Bible was the very Word of God, we would steal away to it constantly. Nothing could keep us away from those precious words. "You mean, God is speaking?" we'd say. "Like . . . God? *The* God? The God who made everything and keeps everything going and holds my destiny in his hand? That God wrote a book? Let me at it!"

If you want to know what God has done and is doing and is going to do, read the Bible. If you want to know how to live and how to love and how to survive and how to thrive, read the Bible. If you want to know what God thinks about you, read the Bible. Here's J. I. Packer again: "Think of the Bible as a listening post where you go to hear the voice of God. . . . In describing the Holy Scripture as a listening post, I am pointing to its instrumentality as the means whereby we are enabled to understand the mind of God toward us."[7] The listening post is so crucial to our engagement in the divine dialogue. Unlike Moses, we won't know what it's like to speak to the Lord as one does with a friend—at least not until we get to heaven and finally see him face-to-face—but by the Spirit's power we do get to be friends with God! We do get to participate in the divine dialogue. The Spirit is speaking to us through his Word when we go to listen, and the Spirit is helping us pray when we go to speak to God.

Your time in the Bible is the primary means by which the Holy Spirit empowers you to live your life. If you don't want this power, by all means, don't go to your Bible. Go to Twitter or Facebook or YouTube. Go to cable news or satellite sports. Go to the movies or a self-help seminar. Go anywhere else if it's not power you're interested in. But if you want to dwell daily in the supernatural realm of God's kingdom and hear *the very words of God*, your Bible is where it's at.

The question most of us have, though, is "How do I do this?" How can you make the most of your daily time in God's Word, tapping into as much of the power in it as you're able? Many times we read our Bibles as if we are in a sailboat but paddling the water with our bare hands. You can do it, but it is not advisable.

Bible study programs and reading schedules abound. Bible memorization systems, study Bibles and devotional books, Bible reading calendars, and other study helps are in vast supply. There are plenty of options to choose from for every temperament and interest. You may find some of these tools helpful. But daily dwelling in God's power isn't about a checklist or a religious program. It's not simply about *what* you're reading but *how* you're reading.

The following five practices may not be new to you (and none were invented by me, of course), but they are generally good disciplines for essential Bible study. Put into intentional practice, these approaches can condition you to *feel* Scripture more keenly, more in step with the Spirit's wisdom within it.

1. Interpret before you apply.

As we bring to Bible study the inherent message of self-centeredness, first asking about a passage of Scripture, "What does this mean *to me*?" becomes natural. We should instead first ask, "What does this passage mean?" This is the practice of interpreting before applying.

Jesus said that if anyone wishes to follow him, he must deny himself and take up his cross (Luke 9:23). When we leap to application first, we immediately diminish the powerful relevance of this teaching. When we apply first, we end up seeing taking up crosses as being about dealing with annoying coworkers or enduring a nagging spouse. But these applications skip the primary meaning: taking up one's cross is about death. This doesn't mean the passage can't apply to annoying coworkers or nagging spouses, but interpreting Luke 9:23 as dying to our own desires helps us apply it to situations with others in selfless ways. An annoying coworker, then, is not someone to endure, but someone to love sacrificially. This makes the Bible come alive—and be felt!—in ways jumping to personal application can't.

At its root, applying before interpreting comes from an assumption that the Bible is not relevant until we make it so. But the Bible is already relevant. It doesn't need us. The Bible is what we truly need, but in our zeal to make it relevant to our wants and needs, we often lose the danger in its primary relevancy. Because Scripture is God's revelation to us, it is imminently and enduringly relevant.

"Interpretation before application" is a fundamental element to all Bible study, but if our desire is to develop a greater feel for Scripture, we will subject our feelings more and more to Scripture's unwavering revelation (interpretation) rather than subject Scripture to our feelings (what often happens in application).

2. Keep it in context.

Here is one area where the effects of consumer culture are really apparent. From CliffsNotes to microwaves, we want everything we do to take as little time and require as little energy as possible. Unfortunately, this desire extends to how we want our Bible served up to us. Even the teaching in many of our churches follows the lead of television news sound bites, giving us a verse or two at a time from different spots in the Bible. You cannot see the beauty of a tapestry if you are only shown a thread at a time.

The result is that over time we lose a sense of the Bible's continuity and larger story. We hear it in little spurts, and it starts to seem to us like a fortune cookie.

Out of context, Jesus' statement "I have not come to bring peace, but a sword" (Matt. 10:34) makes him sound like Conan the Barbarian.

Out of context, Hebrews 6:4–6 seems to indicate that Christians can ultimately "lose" their salvation, but three verses later (Heb. 6:9), the author of Hebrews contrasts what is described in verses 4 through 6 with "better things—things that belong to salvation."

We like to keep Scripture short and manageable, and that's understandable. It's certainly more convenient that way. But we will not be mastered by Scripture and learn to feel it if we don't occasionally allow it to overwhelm us, intimidate us, and force us to wrestle with it. Bite-size chunks are good for memorization and the like, but to feel Scripture, we must drink from it deeply, wade gradually into deeper waters, and do this constantly.

3. Make connections.

Making connections might be the most fun of the practices of feeling Scripture. Although the Bible contains sixty-six books written by about forty authors and covers all kinds of genres, the entire thing is one cohesive story, a brilliant tapestry woven from the same few threads.

One way we can get a better feel for the continuity of Scripture is to make the connections between different passages. All the stories and teachings in the Bible are connected somehow; there are no coincidences. Many connections exist, particularly between the Old Testament and the New Testament, and between Jesus' teaching and the teaching in the New Testament letters, that testify to the premeditation of God's revelation.

For example, read the story in John 6:16–21:

> When evening came, his disciples went down to the sea, got into a boat, and started across the sea to Capernaum. It was now dark, and Jesus had not yet come to them. The sea became rough because a strong wind was blowing. When they had rowed about three or four miles, they saw Jesus walking on the sea and coming near the boat, and they were frightened. But he said to them, "It is I; do not be afraid." Then they were glad to take him into the boat, and immediately the boat was at the land to which they were going.

What are some connections we can make from this story?

The most obvious connection we can make is the parallel narrative in Matthew's gospel (14:22–33). Thinking more deeply, however, we might be able to make other, less obvious connections, such as Jesus' declaration "It is I" recalling God revealing his name in the Old Testament, "I AM." Jesus on the water can remind us of the Spirit hovering over the surface of the deep in the beginning of Genesis. The boat immediately going to the shore when Jesus boarded brings to mind God separating the land from the chaotic waters in the creation story. The story itself reminds us of other stormy sea tales, like that of Noah and the ark, Jonah and the big fish, or even when Jesus slept below deck while the disciples fretted over a storm.

Making connections like this trains our minds to read Scripture as part of one story, and it cultivates in us the ability to feel the breadth of Scripture. Of course this takes more time than just reading a Bible passage and being done with it, but the reward is worth the time. You won't be able to enjoy the sustenance of the Bible if you treat it like a drive-thru window.

I am not saying that what one passage means in one place it also means in a place where you have made a connection. I am only saying that Scripture interprets Scripture, and that the more connections we make, the greater feel we will have for the brilliant unity of the Bible.

As you're reading a particular passage, ask yourself, "What other passages does this remind me of?" Then track those passages down using cross-references or a concordance or an online Bible search program. Before you know it, you will be making connections, and soon enough, you will get a feel for the broader and fuller contours of the Bible's story.

4. Look for Jesus.

Showing you Jesus is what the Holy Spirit is most after in your life. His role is to glorify the Son in our lives and in the world, so that we might be transformed into the Son's likeness. So we read the Bible most in step with the Spirit's inspiration of it when we watch for Christ.

According to Jesus himself in Luke 24:27, the entire Old Testament is about him. Paul echoes this assertion in 2 Corinthians 1:20. Of course, the New Testament is more explicitly about Jesus, as we see the narratives of his earthly ministry in the Gospels and the outworking and application of it in the Epistles. The point is that the entire Bible is making much of Jesus and his saving role in the lives of sinners. If you want to experience the only thing the Bible calls power—the gospel of Jesus Christ—you will be looking for his presence no matter what book of the Bible you're in.

For instance, as I'm reading in Deuteronomy about bodily fluids and ritual cleansing, I can think of how Christ touched the woman who had a bloody discharge for twelve years, healing her and commending her faith. I can thank God in those moments that despite my own religious uncleanliness, Jesus Christ has come near to me and touched me, healing me of my sin and restoring me to union with himself. I can remember that for all the holy weight and godly gravity brought to bear on mankind through the Law, the gospel of Christ is weightier still, and more glorious.

5. Apply prayerfully.

When you're ready to apply Scripture—remember, interpretation comes first—instead of applying a passage in a static sense, apply it in a prayerful, dynamic sense. Here is what I mean by this difference:

First Corinthians 13:7 tells us that "love bears all things." In a static application, we read this and may think, *This is important because my mother is really difficult to live with. She's very burdensome.* In a prayerful application, we read this and turn it into a prayer: *Lord, give me the strength and passion to love my mother even when I find it very difficult. Change my heart to be able to bear all things.*

The first approach is basic application. It is not invalid so far as it goes, but it is distressingly close to subjecting Scripture to our experience rather than vice versa. It is also more observational than it is motivational. It only involves noticing something, not committing to something. Thus, it is static; it lacks movement.

The prayerful approach to application, however, not only presses us to subject our feelings to Scripture—in the example above, the application entails asking God to provide strength for a difficult relationship—but it also turns the application into a conversation with the one prompting the response. Applying prayerfully takes us beyond noticing, "Hey, this reminds me of my problem," to bringing that problem before the Lord and taking the initiative of being changed by Scripture's addressing of that problem.

A static application of 1 Corinthians 13:7 can tempt us to gracelessness, because the focus is on what must be endured (a difficult mother), rather than on the endurance itself. And we can end up with an application that runs counter to the point of the verse in the first place!

In the prayerful application approach, the impetus is toward grace, because the focus is on loving according to the Scripture's call in 1 Corinthians 13. Because of this, the prayerful approach to application is a highly successful way to begin feeling Scripture.

Applying what we read in the Bible is a key component to following Jesus. We aren't simply to read the Word but to *do* it also (James 1:22). But reading comes first! We cannot engage in real, actual friendship with the Spirit of God if we don't listen to him. And because the Spirit speaks primarily, authoritatively, and sufficiently through the Bible, we cannot rightly say that we are listening for God's voice if we don't read the Bible.

Applying *prayerfully* is key as well. We have no power in and of ourselves. The power we need to apply God's Word in ways that honor God and magnify Jesus can only come from God himself. It is in prayer that we "tap into" this power.

Prayer is how we respond to what God has said and play our speaking role in the divine dialogue. Fortunately, as we'll see in our next chapter, the Spirit of the living God has us covered in that area too.

CHAPTER 5

THE SPIRITUAL POWER OF PRAYER

Experiencing the Spirit's Strength

One of the scariest questions I've ever been asked is, "How's your prayer life?"

Most people I know struggle with maintaining a vibrant prayer life. On one level, I find this very discouraging. On another level, I find it very encouraging, since it means I'm not alone! I have, for most of my Christian life, struggled to maintain this vital connection with God. I know I'm supposed to pray—that, actually, I'm supposed to "pray without ceasing" (1 Thess. 5:17)—but most of the time, in the midst of the busyness of my routines, I am unceasing without praying.

Our friend Bill was like that too. Before he pressed "reset" on his life, he usually only thought about prayer during a church service or in another Christian gathering time. Though he spent lots of time in solitude due to his isolated, insulated routine, he very rarely felt prompted to turn his internal monologue toward his Creator. The kinds of information he was consuming didn't seem to stir his need to talk to God.

As with Bible reading, Bill had struggled with regular prayer for most of his Christian life. In fact, he had struggled with prayer more so than with Bible reading, because at least with reading, he could tangibly see a starting and ending point. It is easier with Bible reading to "check off" something accomplished. The hard work of expression has been done for us. The words are already there; we just read them.

But when Bill had previously tried to spend any significant amount of time in prayer, he found himself easily distracted or discouraged. He didn't always know what to say. Sometimes he'd lose his train of thought.

Has this ever happened to you? I'm willing to bet it has.

It is a Sunday at church that helps Bill unlock a substantial part of the puzzle of prayer. The service begins as it always has, with the reading of a Bible passage. In the printed worship guide, Bill sees this reading is labeled "Call to Worship." Now, if Bill had grown up in a more liturgical church setting, he might have been instructed on the meaning of the call to worship, but he didn't, and for whatever reason, he has never really considered the meaning of the different elements of a worship service until this morning.

Suddenly, though, he sees the connection: the Scripture reading is a sort of invitation from God. In the Bible passage each Sunday, God is speaking through his Word, calling out for response. The worship time immediately after constitutes the congregation's response to what God has said.

The "dialogical" shape of the worship service appears to Bill for the first time. And he thinks to himself, *Prayer is like this.*

In a sense, prayer is "talking back" to God. No, it's not talking back in the sarcastic or disrespectful sense. It is a response. God has spoken in his Word. God has spoken in our hearts. God has spoken in his converting us to Christ by his Holy Spirit. So in prayer we respond to all these lines of divine inquiry. We pray to thank God for his Word and to ask him to help us understand and apply it. We pray to thank God for loving us and for establishing his kingdom on earth. We pray to thank God for sending his Son to die and rise for us and to "renew" continuously the gospel in our lives. We pray to ask for forgiveness and for help with repenting of our sin and loving our neighbors.

Prayer is, fundamentally, our way of participating in the divine dialogue begun by the Spirit in the Bible. It is helpful to think of prayer this way because it demystifies prayer a bit and makes it more practical and thus more doable. It also helps us guard against unbiblical thinking about prayer and its impact in our world.

Indeed, some Christians need a reformation of their views on the Spiritual power of prayer precisely because their current views owe too much to (lowercase *s*) spirituality that does not come from the Holy Spirit himself.

Prayer Is Not Magic

The way some people talk about prayer owes more to New Age ideology and witchcraft than biblical Christianity—that is, they envision prayer as a mystical tool for harnessing energy and manipulating reality to achieve certain life goals they have set for themselves. In the world of the occult, spells are cast and chants are conducted to wield a certain kind of man-centered power. I'm afraid too many Christians think of prayers in ways that are not markedly different from this! I'll give you one concrete example of errant teaching on prayer sometimes found in the church.

I don't want to name any names, but I recall when I was a teenager being taught about "spiritual warfare" in ways I cannot seem to find supported in the Bible. Sometimes God and Satan were cast as warring opposites, a kind of yin and yang balancing each other out even while squaring off. Which side will win in the battle for your soul and the fate of the universe? Well, whichever side you support, of course.

Such thinking sounds really stupid and blasphemous. But books, songs, and movies were made for the evangelical subculture that reflected just that kind of warped theology of the spiritual plane. Jesus almost became a version of Tinkerbell, needing our "applause" to gain strength and prevail over the enemy.

This sort of man-centered spirituality is at the heart of the modern-day prosperity gospel, particularly in the strain known as "word of faith." Promoters of this empty view regularly encourage followers to speak only positive words and warn them against bringing curses upon themselves with negative attitudes. Do you want health, wealth, and prosperity? Name them and claim them. Do you want to ward off disease and disaster? The power of your tongue can rebuke their impact on your life.

All this spiritual hoo-ha mistakes the very real presence of Spiritual power in the Christian's life as there for the glory of us rather than the glory of God. One only needs to read through the book of Acts, where we see both the mighty works of the

Holy Spirit on vivid display in the life of the early church along-side the frequent imprisonments, beatings, interrogations, and even executions of early Christians, to see that the Spirit's mighty working in our lives does not preclude the experience of some extreme kinds of suffering.

By all means, pray big prayers and expect God to come through, but remember that prayer isn't magic.

When some Christians talk about the "power of prayer," one gets the impression that they believe there is some force inherent in our words, sourced in ourselves, that can make or break reality. The "name it and claim it" crowd operates as if the one praying is in control rather than the one being prayed to.

Is prayer powerful? Yes, definitely, but specifically because the one being prayed to is powerful. The one doing the praying is, by her praying, demonstrating that she has no power in and of herself. That is functionally what prayer is—an expression of helplessness. If we were powerful, we wouldn't need to pray.

James said that "the prayer of a righteous person has great power as it is working" (5:16), so we need to take great care to notice that "as it is working" gives a shape to the prayer. Literally, this verse can be expressed this way: "the prayers that work"—or, "the effective prayers"—"have great power." This tells us two things. First, some prayers don't "work." By this, I assume it is meant that we don't always get what we ask for when we pray. We may ask God to satisfy a certain desire or heal a certain wound. Sometimes he says no. But second, we notice that the prayers that have effect have great power. Where could that come from?

If you said *you*, go sit in the corner.

But you didn't say that, did you? You know where great

power comes from. You know when you're frustrated in traffic, irritated with your family, triggered by a reminder of your past, tripped up by a recurring sin, or depressed by an inconsolable loneliness that "great power" is not something that comes to you naturally. It isn't found "within"—at least, not within your natural self.

No, the power that effective prayer has is nothing and nobody less than the Holy Spirit of God, who not only hears the prayer but carries the prayer and replies to the prayer and even inspires the prayer!

But let's take it a step further. Prayer isn't magic because we have no power in and of ourselves. Prayer is expressed helplessness. But also, prayer isn't magic because God isn't helpless without our moving him or unleashing him or activating him in some way. I cringe every time I hear some well-intentioned preacher use the phrase "let God"—as in, "You have to let God take control of your life" and "You need to let God be God."

First of all, God doesn't need you to let him do anything. He isn't restrained or controlled by you. God isn't like some tethered toddler on a parental leash at the mall, struggling for freedom to have at the world around him. What saps we are if we think we have the power to "let God" do anything. He's God. We're not. Period.

So in prayer you are not commanding the Spirit or summoning the Spirit like he's a cosmic butler. In prayer you are not in the place of control but in the place of submission. In a previous book I called prayer "spilling your guts,"[1] because it is through prayer that we bare our hearts, minds, and souls to the God who wants to be our Friend. And the more we do this baring, the more we will experience his power, even in our lowest and weakest moments.

Prayer isn't magic. Prayer in practice is simply talking to God. We don't need to make it more complicated than that. Of course, prayer is heavy-duty stuff; it is the act by which we say, "Here I am," in response to God calling our name, our peeking up from behind the bushes à la Adam and Eve in response to God's "Where are you?"

Prayer is the act that, through Jesus and by the Holy Spirit, puts us in the open embrace of the Father who listens with love. You can kneel, you can stand, you can sit, you can recline. You can clasp your hands or lift them. You can bow your head or raise it to heaven. You can close your eyes or behold creation. You can pray aloud or in your head. However you go about it, you can't complicate the act itself by ignoring the simplicity that all of it is *talking to God*.

I think once many of us realize that prayer is simply talking to God, it starts to seem easier to do. Paul tells us never to stop praying (1 Thess. 5:17), but there are still many of us who have trouble finding the rhythm of prayer in noisy, compartmentalized lives. Below are some exercises that may or may not be new to you but nevertheless may help you pick up the rhythm of prayer that once begun can take on a life of its own in your daily abiding in Jesus.

1. Praying written prayers.

Sometimes words are hard to find. Or after they've come, we find frustration in repeating ourselves. If your prayers feel "stale," you may be interested in praying words written by others. This practice can be done in a rote and faithless manner, but many times praying prewritten prayers helps us find new ways into prayer, reminds us of things we had not thought to pray for, or leads us to discover our own words on similar subjects. There is nothing magical or mystical about praying prewritten prayers, but neither is there anything shameful or remedial in it. Reading written words as prayers to God can be a great help for those who struggle with a wandering mind or lack of vocabulary. Numerous devotional and prayer books are available that can help in this regard. One of the best is *The Valley of Vision*, a classic work of Puritan prayers and devotions, all of which are drenched in kingdom focus and centered on God's glory.

Of course, with written prayers you will need to be discerning about theological and spiritual content, as well as about whether the feelings expressed authentically apply to you. But then those are discernments we must make in prayers "off the top of the head" as well.

2. Praying Scripture.

If written prayers seem like your kind of thing, there's no better source of writing to pray than the Word of God itself. The Psalms, which run the gamut of the human experience, are the likeliest place to find heartfelt, God-exalting prayers, but any Scripture can be prayed if you can think through applying it prayerfully as part of the rhythm of feeling Scripture.

3. Wandering prayer.

The great thing about our God is that he takes us as we are but does not leave us as he finds us. This means that a wandering mind (and even body) is okay in prayer. If you are engaged in the practice of intentional prayer in solitude and quiet, God, who is outside of time, is not offended if it takes you time to get everything expressed or you have to wander around your house or neighborhood or park to clear yourself of noise. There is nothing magical about staying in one place or staying on one track mentally. You may begin with many words and slowly run out, but if you are drawing close to God, stay there and think.

Let your mind wander and then find its way back to prayer. There is no such thing as perfect prayer. Jesus is perfect, and he bears the burden of perfection in prayer for you. Walk around. Sing. Read. Intersperse prayer with devotional reading or Bible study. Talk to yourself a bit. Work out the kinks. It's okay. God can handle "messy."

4. Journaling prayer.

If you have trouble staying focused and want help with staying on track, one of the best practices to engage in is writing down your prayers. Instead of verbalizing your prayers, write them out. This will keep you on track. And it has the added benefit of your being able to look back and see snapshots of your devotional life over time.

Many times even as we unplug from the noise of life, find a place of quiet solitude, and engage in prayer, we still have difficulty achieving rhythm in prayer because we are attempting a form that feels artificial or forced. Written prayers, scriptural prayers, wandering prayers, and journaled prayers are all ways to breathe new life into your time of intentional prayer. Perhaps the newness of one of these ways or the alternating of a variety of these ways can help you regain the rhythm of intimate conversation with God.

One way to kill your prayer life is to overthink it. The best friendships you and I have are with people with whom we feel we can be ourselves. We feel most "at home" with the friends we don't feel self-conscious around. This doesn't mean that you can't or shouldn't plan your prayers or schedule time for prayer. It just means that the most vibrant prayer lives are found in those who are willing to bring their whole selves to God, to be themselves before God, for better or worse. And the beautiful mystery of this exchange—our emptiness for God's fullness—is that the Holy Spirit is inspiring and sustaining the whole thing. Talk about experiencing Spiritual power!

The Empowered Prayer

Prayer is expressed helplessness. And prayer is an experience of strength. How can both of these statements be true?

Well there is, of course, the way the Holy Spirit replies to our expressed helplessness with his strong response. But one little-considered way the natural work of prayer demonstrates the supernatural power of God is where prayer comes from in the first place. Here's what I mean:

Have you ever pondered how the requirement to pray fits into God's sovereign plan for the world? I mean, if you believe, as correct-thinking Christians do, that God is in control and that he knows all things that are going to happen—he sees the future, in other words—why is it that you pray?

Why do we ask God to do certain things if the decision to do (or not to do) them has already been determined anyway? Doesn't this make our prayer kind of pointless? Some people ask why, if God is in control, do we pray at all? But really we have this question upside down.

Pastor John Piper has offered a helpful explanation to the *why* of Christian prayer in the face of God's certain knowledge of the future in this dazzling little dialogue:

Prayerless: I understand that you believe in the
  providence of God. Is that right?

Prayerful: Yes.

Prayerless: Does that mean you believe . . . that
  nothing comes about by chance but only by God's
  design and plan?

Prayerful: Yes, I believe that's what the Bible teaches.

Prayerless: Then why do you pray?

Prayerful: I don't see the problem. Why shouldn't we
  pray?

Prayerless: Well, if God ordains and controls
  everything, then what he plans from of old will
  come to pass, right?

Prayerful: Yes.

Prayerless: So it's going to come to pass whether you
  pray or not, right?

Prayerful: That depends on whether God ordained
  for it to come to pass in answer to prayer. If God
  predestined that something happen in answer to
  prayer, it won't happen without prayer.

Prayerless: Wait a minute, this is confusing. Are you
  saying that every answer to prayer is predestined or
  not?

Prayerful: Yes, it is. It's predestined as an answer to
  prayer.

Prayerless: So if the prayer doesn't happen, the answer
  doesn't happen?

Prayerful: That's right.

Prayerless: So the event is contingent on our praying
  for it to happen?

Prayerful: Yes. I take it that by contingent you mean prayer is a real reason that the event happens, and without the prayer the event would not happen.

Prayerless: Yes, that's what I mean. But how can an event be contingent on my prayer and still be eternally fixed and predestined by God?

Prayerful: Because your prayer is as fixed as the predestined answer.

Prayerless: Explain.

Prayerful: It's not complicated. God providentially ordains all events. God never ordains an event without a cause. The cause is also an event. Therefore, the cause is also foreordained. So you cannot say that the event will happen if the cause doesn't because God has ordained otherwise. The event will happen if the cause happens.[2]

Even our prayers are predestined!

I don't know what you think of that—what your view on predestination is—but I find it extremely encouraging, if only because I see my prayer life as a cultivated fruit of God's Spirit working in me. If God's Spirit really is sanctifying me, why wouldn't I expect a developing prayer life to be a part of that?

Truly, though, if you're a Christian serious about praying, you already have a default view of God's sovereignty in the world. J. I. Packer explains:

I do not intend to spend any time at all proving to you the general truth that God is sovereign in His world. There is no need; for I know that, if you are a Christian, you believe this already.

How do I know that? Because I know that, if you are a Christian, you pray; and the recognition of God's sovereignty is the basis of your prayers. In prayer, you ask for things and give thanks for things. Why? Because you recognize that God is the author and source of all the good that you have had already, and all the good that you hope for in the future. This is the fundamental philosophy of Christian prayer. The prayer of a Christian is not an attempt to force God's hand, but a humble acknowledgment of helplessness and dependence. When we are on our knees, we know that it is not we who control the world; it is not in our power, therefore, to supply our needs by our own independent efforts; every good thing that we desire for ourselves and for others must be sought from God, and will come, if it comes at all, as a gift from His hands.[3]

In other words, why pray if God *isn't* in control?

How incredible is it simply to consider that our prayers can be effectual to work wonders in the world because our prayers themselves are the effects of God's work in the world? It may not be a complicated idea, as Piper said, but it is certainly a staggering one!

Our prayers are empowered by God. What a concept.

If thinking along those lines is difficult for you intellectually or theologically, think not simply of the predestined nature of your prayer but of the privileged nature of it. If it's true that the Spirit empowers our prayers as causes to God-ordained events, it means we puny humans get the awesome privilege of participating in God's work in the world. The power does not come from us, but it can work *through* us.

Praying is our way of participating in the divine life. Praying is our way of responding to God's initiative in the divine dialogue.

Walking by Faith

Bill's perspective on his entire world is changing. Where before he might have seen Bible study and prayer as important parts of his life, he saw them as just that—*parts* of *his* life. But as he has come to follow the Spirit's conviction about his compartmentalized life, he is seeing that all he has and all he is happens to be the outworking of God's plan for God's own glory in the world. So hearing from God through the Bible is bigger than simply discovering some religious guidance or personal pick-me-ups for the week. It involves hearing the secret workings of heaven set loose in the everyday stuff of earth.

Bill's ordinary little prayers are therefore functioning like gears in the mechanism of the kingdom God is establishing in the world. As Jesus himself instructed us to pray, "Your kingdom come, your will be done, on earth as it is in heaven" (Matt. 6:10).

Bill reads the Lord's Prayer in his journey through Matthew's gospel, and while he was familiar with it before, it strikes him newly as big and glorious and supernatural. If he really is going to withstand temptation and forgive those who hurt him and even just survive each day, he is going to have to submit more and more of himself to the power of the Spirit. And the good news for the praying Christian is that he is already experiencing the Spirit's power, right there in his prayers.

Just as the worship service Bill experienced was a response to the biblical call to worship, Bill begins to see his own life as a prayer of sorts, a response to the biblical call to follow Jesus. Thus, prayer becomes more integral to his life, a larger expression of his ongoing need. The more Bill is in touch with his absolute need for the Spirit's power, the more he finds himself asking for it. He becomes a better "pray-er" when he becomes a more will-ing "surrenderer."

As we walk by faith and not by sight, prayer helps us respond to the Lord's voice in the Bible with submission and trust.

For my own part, I am trusting as I read through, say, Deuteronomy, that the Spirit is doing something with it I can-not see. In the immediacy of my reading and in the overarching anxieties of my daily life, I cannot see how reading about what to do with discharges of bodily fluid helps me at all! But I am trusting. I am trusting that the Spirit is using it to build me up in secret. I mean, I don't know anything, really, about the inner workings of DNA. And if you tried to explain it to me, I might get more confused. But I know that even the stuff I don't under-stand makes me *me*.

When Jesus was resurrected, he appeared to his disciples in a locked room. Thomas said, "I won't believe unless I can touch your wounds." The merciful Christ allowed Thomas's touch. And yet, with his coming ascension in mind, Jesus said to Thomas, "Have you believed because you have seen me? Blessed are those who have not seen and yet have believed" (John 20:29). Jesus was reminding Thomas—as us—that the righteous do not walk by sight, but by faith.

You don't need a miracle. You need a word from God. And out of the abundance of his grace, God has provided sixty-six books of them.

So the divine dialogue is our way of staying connected to the supernatural power at work in the world and in our lives. God has come near. His Spirit has indwelled us and his Spirit is still speaking to us. He speaks to us in his Word, and we respond to him in prayer. As I suggested earlier, there may be other ways for us to engage in this dialogue, but we don't need them like we need this way. And anyone eager to move past prayer and Bible study hasn't really succeeded at prayer and Bible study.

Theologians call Bible study and prayer "means of grace"—meaning they are key ways that God imparts his favor to us through the power of his Spirit. Other means of grace available to us: receiving baptism at conversion, participating in communion at church with God's family, hearing the preaching of the Word in a sermon, even simply participating in loving fellowship with the body of Christ. But for seeking the kind of power we need to get through and get by in our daily lives, the ordinary means of grace come through this extraordinary privilege of divine dialogue. We talk to God, and he talks to us.

We are divided (compartmentalized) about God, but he is not divided about us. The reality of the divine dialogue is proof that all of the Godhead is at work in our lives. Just as we are saved because of the Father's commission, the Son's atonement, and the Spirit's regeneration, we continue to partake in the very nature of God because of the Father's enduring love, the Son's eternal righteousness, and the Spirit's enlightening power. All of the Trinity is on deck! We may want to put God in some religious box in our modern life, but the Ancient of Days is rejoicing over us and listening to us at all times. "The great comfort in this," Joe Thorn wrote, "is not that he simply hears you, but that you have his undivided attention."[4]

And so we may not be able to see God. Not yet, anyway. But we can know God. We can hear God. His Spirit is speaking to us, drawing us near, holding us close, imparting the love of the Father through the blood of the Son to our hearts and minds. We can trust this is happening even if we don't see it or feel it. We can walk by faith.

We can walk by faith, not by sight, because the Holy Spirit we cannot see is enabling us to do so by his great power.

CHAPTER 6

THE BLESSING OF GOING WITHOUT

Experiencing the Spirit's Filling

Once upon a time, I found myself on the receiving end of some arched eyebrows and uncomfortable chuckles while speaking at a church conference. I had had the audacity to criticize the city where the conference was being hosted to an audience made up mostly of its citizens. Where was I?

Ocean City, New Jersey. Which I quite enjoyed, actually.

I was really just trying to be funny. You see, Ocean City has an unbelievable seaside boardwalk that stretches for miles. But the little businesses that line the boardwalk are not what you'd typically expect to find on the Jersey shore, or really any vacation beach area. Ocean City is known for its family-friendly atmosphere. So while along the boardwalk you can find countless pizza joints, funnel cake shops, gift stores, mini-golf courses, and assorted and sundry other touristy attractions, you won't find much in the way of bars or nightclubs or other kinds of places you might not want your children to see.

So I offered the conference crowd a backhanded compliment, quipping that I had enjoyed a long walk that afternoon through their "family-friendly Vanity Fair." The groans were audible.

Vanity Fair is the attraction John Bunyan's Christian finds himself navigating a few chapters deep into the classic allegory *The Pilgrim's Progress*. Based on Bunyan's own recollections of a lavish exhibition near Cambridge, the setting in his book represents the seductive and tantalizing excesses of the culture, which are used by the Enemy to distract and subsume Christian in worldliness.

The symbol of Vanity Fair endures to this day, as the root of Bunyan's concern is clearly biblical. James 4:4 is just one example of a warning about the temptations of worldly comforts. But so is almost the entire book of Ecclesiastes and large swaths of the prophetic books in the Old Testament.

Many of the world's temptations are easy to spot. All true Christians will recognize the dangers of pornography and other explicitly sexual immorality. And nearly everyone recognizes the dangers of alcohol and drug addiction. But some worldly temptations are much subtler, wilier, and Christians have not fared so well.

This is why I think the family-friendly Vanity Fairs are more dangerous. They don't exhibit an obvious danger, just a little bit of harmless, frivolous fun. We dip our toes into the water, and before long we are neck-deep in conspicuous consumption. Greed, gluttony, envy—these are harder sins to spot. They are especially harder to spot in Western evangelicalism, where we've even begun to craft our church experiences according to the flavors found in the Vanity Fair.

It is remarkable to me how so many of the congregations that market themselves as "Spirit-filled churches" actually seem filled with something else—namely, the spirit of materialism. We model our buildings after shopping centers, our gatherings after rock concerts, and our ministries after secular corporations. We emphasize consumer "felt needs" and custom-ordered desires. Many of our churches, in fact, have become their own family-friendly Vanity Fairs. Even some churches that advertise "authentic," "relevant," and "dynamic" spiritual encounters work hard in their own efforts to produce these effects. If your marquee says "Spirit-Filled Church" but your entire ministry says "spirit of the age," you're doing it wrong.

How can we say with any integrity that we long for the Spirit to fill us when we are constantly drinking at the well of culture and feasting at the table of worldliness? As we saw in the previous chapter, the primary and normative way the Spirit speaks to us—feeds us—is through God's infallible Word. So when we go off chasing some spiritual high apart from his Word, seeking out "worship experiences" and looking for extra-biblical signs and wonders, we don't "unleash" the Spirit; we're actually seeking to cage him! The prosperity gospel *quenches* the Spirit of God.

The real devil in the details of the prosperity-type teaching you see on religious television and on too many Christian bookstore shelves is not really that it skips over the stuff about sin. Sure, it does that too. But the pernicious paradox of this stuff is that it champions "victorious Christian living" yet does not equip believers for a sustainable life as a Christian. It emphasizes feelings and "outlook" rather than the power of the Spirit, which is hard for some folks to notice since the latter is often conflated with the former (so that being optimistic or a go-getter is ipso facto being Spirit empowered).

The problem with this over time is that, going from victory to victory, expecting victory after victory, cultivates a contagious form of spiritual greed and gluttony. (Is it any wonder that this sort of teaching often goes hand in hand with talk of financial riches and "the good life"?) The real stuff of discipleship—what Eugene Peterson calls "a long obedience in the same direction"[1]— involves hard stuff like discipline and the fruit of the Spirit. In pop discipleship, discipline is replaced by steps, tips, and *amazing, supercolossal* breakthroughs.

When my children were tiny, we had in our household a couple of "Laws of Raising Children." The first law is no item in the universe is more interesting than the one a sibling is currently holding. The second law is no matter where you are (and it could be Disney World), there is some other place you'd rather be.

Getting what we don't have, being somewhere we aren't— that defines the childishness of the children in our house. But they are *children*, so they have an excuse.

The prosperity gospel, then, which promises an abundantly fulfilling life, ironically breeds discontentment. It feeds on the immaturity of the need for immediate gratification, never simply *abiding* with God where we are, because we always consider what we have less than what's available (or at least less than what our neighbor has). We always think of today as less than tomorrow.

But you cannot get to resurrection day without going through the cross.

There's a fine line between contentment and complacency,

also, and I think this implicit confusion is why contentment is rarely spoken of these days. You'll never catch prosperity gospelists praying for contentment; to them this would imply stagnation or laziness. But contentment isn't about not caring; contentment is about caring for the needs of the moment. It is about obedience and faith. Paul was not complacent about his repeated imprisonment and torture. But, amazingly enough, he was content.

Contentment trusts God to be God. Discontentment, on the other hand, reveals our fear of everything *but* God—fears of lack of safety, of financial insolvency, of what others might think of us, even of "spiritual immaturity." The content soul, however, fears God (Prov. 19:23). Paul even said that it is the kind of godliness that comes with contentment, not consumption, that is something worth having (1 Tim. 6:6).

The great irony of the prosperity gospel is that it actually cultivates its own need for itself. It is built on discontent and gluttony and desire (whether for stuff or for "spirituality"), and therefore it turns in on itself, self-perpetuating, continuing to create the needs it promises to fill. We all know what happens when you try to fill a God-shaped void with anything not God shaped. We all know that money doesn't buy happiness. But contentment! Being content with what we have, with where God has us, whether it be on top of a mountain surrounded by beauty or down in a valley walking toward a pit we cannot see—now that is true gain!

But there are no easy steps to contentment. The word *content* evokes feelings of peace and tranquility, of being carefree. And those things are true, in a sense. But the way to contentment is difficult, and the place of contentment itself may be in a harsh and barren land. That is, after all, how you know you've reached contentment. Being content involves the tough stuff of trust and discipline and obedience and biblical love. As G. K. Chesterton once said, "True contentment is a thing as active as agriculture. It is the power of getting out of any situation all that there is in it. It is arduous and it is rare."[2]

I think this is why the Bible connects contentment so often to times of suffering and difficulty, not times of comfort and ease. Our sense of settled-in satisfaction comes not from our outward circumstances but from the inner reality of the Spirit's work. Indeed, we find that the Spirit often leads us into difficulty in order to help us find our contentment in Christ alone. Christians are people compelled to believe that "God loves you and has a difficult plan for your life."

So how do we reach contentment? We start where we are, not looking ahead to what is next. We begin with a hope for deliverance, provided we are really in need of it, but also with a trust that God is refining us through the circumstances in which he has presently placed us. It is just that—being *present*. Show up, in this moment, for submission to God. Wave the white flag. Trust that the cross you are bearing is not the end of his story, but accept that cross as necessary and get everything out of it that is there to get.

Our old friend Bill discovered that his circumstantial ease and environmental comforts gradually weren't cutting it for him any longer. He had gotten a taste of the work of the Spirit, and this taste began to dull his appetite for the things of the world. Even some good things Bill had accomplished—the products and achievements of working hard and honestly—became not *bad* but less the center of his trust and satisfaction. And once Bill began to wake up to the reality that all his money, possessions, and lifestyle arrangements couldn't be taken to heaven with him, he became more disillusioned with the promises of contentment the world seemed to make through them.

There are no formulaic steps or aphoristic strategies for contentment. Just the Spirit and the power he gives by his good pleasure. You cannot attain a necessary discontentment with your own achievements all by yourself. You will need the convicting, chastening God of love.

"I know what it is to have little," Paul wrote, "and I know what it is to have plenty. In any and all circumstances I have learned the secret of being well-fed and of going hungry, of having plenty and of being in need. I can do all things through him who strengthens me" (Phil. 4:12–13 NRSV). We don't find our strength in the stuff of the world; we find it in the work of the Spirit. But to be filled with the Spirit and learn this supernatural contentment, we must often be emptied by the Spirit of all else that might satisfy. This chapter is about cooperating with self-denial to experience Spiritual satisfaction.

Fasting Isn't About Food

The kingdom of God runs counter to the way of the world. And it takes some mental and emotional adjustment—powered by a Spiritual adjustment—to see that in fact it is the world that runs counter to God's kingdom. He's not going opposite; the world is! So when Jesus says, "Deny yourself," the denial he commands is ironically about being filled and fulfilled. The consumer world that invites us to gorge ourselves daily on food, news, entertainment, sex, drugs or alcohol, work, reputation, notoriety, money, and all sorts of other things is really just inviting us to be satisfied with anything other than Jesus.

Bill was beginning to realize this truth in his own life. He wasn't trying to stiff-arm the Spirit with his intake of everything else; he was just minding his own business. But because we are fallen creatures with sinful hearts, going on autopilot will always lead us into idolatry.

The problem with the cultural advancements around us isn't necessarily that everything is convenient, comfortable, and casual, but that our routine swimming in these things acclimates us to convenience, comfort, and casualness, none of which are conducive to the life of discipleship that is abiding in Christ. Following Jesus just isn't convenient, comfortable, or casual. It is crucifixion. And this is why too many Christians have opted for a safer faith (complete with safer churches specializing in a safer gospel). The pursuit of the American dream has edged in on the territory of the pursuit of God.

As the story in John 6 goes, the crowds loved it when Jesus was handing out fish and crackers, but once he started talking about subsisting on his body and blood, they scrammed. When Jesus later asked his disciples if they wanted to leave him as well (John 6:67–68), Peter replied, "Lord, to whom shall we go?" These days many may answer, "Well, Bed Bath & Beyond *is* having its white sale right now. . . ."

In a world whose modus operandi is conspicuous consumption, going without can look downright weird and sometimes stupid. Living the kingdom of God in a world of materialism is a call to living simply in the land of the supersized. While the spirit of the age calls us to bigger, better, and more, the gospel of the kingdom leads us to empty ourselves, to find fulfillment in forgoing.

If you have any experience with fasting, it is likely with food. Or perhaps you've given up something like coffee or the Internet for Lent. But fasting isn't just about food, and it is not only about a temporary reset; it is about giving up things by choice. It is a lifestyle do-over. It is part of the big reset we discussed in chapter 3. Further, fasting is about giving up things by choice *for the purpose of a greater fulfillment.*

Few of us ever have to go without things we need, and most of us rarely go without things we want. Nevertheless, when we do go without something, it is typically the latest gadget or trinket that we have decided we can't afford. In those instances, we are not really fasting, because we still want the thing but have just decided we *can't* have it. The sort of "fasting" that prevents us from buying the $300 video game console or pair of shoes is not an act of worship but an act of reason. Our affections are still with the item even if its enjoyment is not with us.

The reason fasting isn't really about food is the same reason our appetite for the iPhone is not really because it's cool. There's nothing wrong with food or iPhones or video games or shoes. So our desire for these things and our need to fast from these things does not mean these things are tainted or sinful in themselves; rather, our desire and need to fast means that *we* are tainted and sinful. Is gluttony a sin because food is evil? Is pornography sinful because sex is in itself bad? No, gluttony and pornography are wrong because they take good things and make them *god* things. They ascribe more worth to food and sex than God does, place hope in food and sex for fulfillment, and ask food and sex to satisfy desires that food and sex are not designed to satisfy (loneliness, depression, angst, discouragement, meaning). Gluttony and pornography (and every other sin) take God's good creation and make it the center of idolatrous religion.

The same is true with our materialistic environments. Our comfortable neighborhoods, for instance, are not bad; nor are people outside God's will for living in them. But the values of the consumers in the modernized West often are the result of taking good things and making them *god* things, seeking fulfillment of needs and appetites in all the goods and services the consumer world has to offer. This idolatry is the root of alcoholism and drug addiction, pornography, greed, and more culturally acceptable sins like gluttony, materialism, and "retail therapy." The religious architecture of this idolatry creates the line between merely consuming goods and services (which is itself a neutral act) and consuming goods and services in appeasement of spiritual or emotional appetites. Idolatrous consumption feeds the consumer culture in which we're not just buying products but whatever promises the products make. (Did you know that the phrase "bad breath" was unknown in popular culture until Listerine was invented?[3])

The culture of consumerism appeals to our spiritual senses, and when our spiritual senses are engaged, we buy in. Whatever gets most of your energy, thought, and desire—that is your god. And if that is true, then fasting for most of us does not mean going without chocolate for a month, but rather, assassinating our idols.

As Jesus outlined the blueprint of the kingdom in the Sermon on the Mount, he cut into this very issue with laserlike precision. "Do not lay up for yourselves treasures on earth, where moth and rust destroy and where thieves break in and steal, but lay up for yourselves treasures in heaven, where neither moth nor rust destroys and where thieves do not break in and steal. For where your treasure is, there your heart will be also" (Matt. 6:19–21).

Jesus pulled the facade off the foolishness of idolatry with its temporary treasures. Your house may be awesome, but it can be burned to the ground. Your car may be fancy, but it's going to rust. Your cell phone may let you track the progress of the Mars rover, but your cell phone (and the Mars rover) will someday be dust. And yet we treat these things with the reverence befitting a permanence they do not have. We pour our thoughts, physical energy, emotions, hopes, and lots and lots of our finances into things that will break down, fall apart, get stolen, or—most commonly—be obsolete in a year.

Instead, Jesus commanded those who abide in his kingdom to treasure permanent things, things with eternal value. And then he honed in on the root of all our consumeristic dysfunction: idolatry. "For where your treasure is, there your heart will be also."

Whatever you are treasuring possesses your heart.

The Importance of Enough

Our failure to fast from crass consumerism stems from our failure to say, "Enough." For those hooked on the drugs of materialism and consumption, there is no such thing as enough. Instead, our mantra is "More," a command that by definition cannot be satisfied. Fasting from anything is a sign that we are denying "More" and saying "Enough."

As we have just learned, though, the reason we had trouble saying "Enough" in the first place is because of the appetites of our flesh and desires of our heart: our spiritual senses. Just because we fast from things that do not satisfy our spiritual senses does not mean we have tamed our senses or that they somehow go into hibernation. To truly say "Enough," we have to experience satisfaction of our spiritual senses. And the only person who truly satisfies is Jesus Christ himself.

In the middle of the Beatitudes we find this central tenet of the kingdom: "Blessed are those who hunger and thirst for righteousness, for they shall be satisfied" (Matt. 5:6). Only God's kingdom is broadcasting on the frequency to which our spiritual senses are tuned. Nothing else satisfies our inward groaning for righteousness. Psalm 42:1 (NRSV) speaks to this perfect fit, as David cried: "As a deer longs for flowing streams, so my soul longs for you, O God."

We take that longing, however, and instead of seeing satisfaction in the living water of God, we try out the toxic sludge of whatever is offered outside the kingdom. We read that verse and don't see our means to assassinating idols but a nice thought to slap on a coffee mug below a picture of a deer and sell for $9.95 at the Christian bookstore.

This hungering and thirsting for righteousness, this panting of our soul for water, is the seeking of our spiritual senses for a larger sense, for the completion of our longing, for the great metronome that has set the *tick-tock* of our insidest insides. In short, we are a spiritual instrument aching from artificial rhythms, aching for true Spiritual rhythms.

Fasting is one of these rhythms, a crucial one, in fact, because it involves repenting from the weight of all that slows us down. Fasting is a rhythm in the same way that *not fasting* is a rhythm. It is the way we live in service to something outside of ourselves. As we saw above, the big house isn't necessarily a bad thing, but orienting your life around paying for, building, and maintaining a big house can be a bad thing. We make sacrifices already; we are just making them for stuff. The rhythms of our life already portray our willingness to go without things like wise financial management, time to rest, anonymity, and even our health in order to get what we want. And those sacrifices are silly! All the rhythm of fasting asks us to do is sacrifice for better, permanent, more fulfilling things.

The late comedian George Carlin was an angry guy who mocked the very idea of God, but even he understood the superficial fulfillment of consumerism. One of his most famous routines involved the relation of the American dream to "stuff." Carlin mused that we buy a home so that our stuff will fit in it, but then we proceed to "need" a bigger home because our accumulation of stuff doesn't end. "That's all a house is," he said, "a place to keep your stuff while you're out getting more stuff." Even the biggest house is not big enough to contain the fruit of conspicuous consumption.

Meanwhile Jesus draws near and—ready to rebuke materialism (Luke 12:33) and rescue the weary (Matt. 11:28)—stands over us with arms outstretched, and to all of us moving to the rhythm of "More," he shouts, "Enough!"

False Fasting

We must return to the difference between "doing" and "being" now, because the temptation we face in reading the Beatitudes and the rest of the Sermon on the Mount is to put on the behavioral expectations like a costume and play a religious part without undergoing any heart change at all, which is frankly how millions of Christians live their lives. Jesus himself called us out on this by speaking specifically on fasting in the sermon:

> "When you fast, do not look gloomy like the hypocrites, for they disfigure their faces that their fasting may be seen by others. Truly, I say to you, they have received their reward. But when you fast, anoint your head and wash your face, that your fasting may not be seen by others but by your Father who is in secret. And your Father who sees in secret will reward you." (Matt. 6:16–18)

Jesus warned against behavioral alignment with the kingdom that lacks heart alignment. To *act* humble is not necessarily to *be* humble.

When we skim this powerful truth, it seems reasonable enough. None of us likes hypocritical people. None of us likes people who pretend to be something they're not. And none of us wants to be those people. But the way Jesus commands humble fasting cuts right to the heart of pretense. He actually encourages "keeping up appearances" as a means of not keeping up appearances. Jesus tells those who fast to clean themselves up a bit. Fix your hair, shave, put on some deodorant. Why?

Because trying to look like you're fasting is as fake as trying to look like you have it all together. The difference is not appearances but attitudes. The difference is the heart.

If studying this book and trying to resemble what it suggests is all an exercise in looking more spiritual, you will have missed the point. The whole point of abiding in Christ according to the rhythms of the kingdom is that life is found outside of your efforts and the rhythms do not originate with you. You can study your Bible, pray, fast, give to charity, and go to church all you want, but if your deeds are not the work of a heart for God, the prophet Isaiah calls them "filthy rags" (Isa. 64:6 NIV).

The New Testament church at various times had to ward off the infiltration of a group of heretics called ascetics. (Paul's letter to the Colossians, for instance, offers instruction in response to the threat of self-righteous asceticism.) Ascetics were those who abstained from certain food or drink, who disengaged from the wider culture, and who adopted rigorous religious disciplines in pursuit of transcendence, enlightenment, or holiness. The bottom line is that for these guys, fasting was the end, not a means to the end. Ascetics trusted their own works to merit salvation.

Joyful fasting is not about asceticism or performance, either to impress God or to impress others. Fasting is a *posture*—a posture of denial we take toward the consumer offerings of the world and of submission toward the loving care and provision of God.

True Fasting

This kingdom rhythm is called "joyful fasting" because the true posture of self-denial is joy. If we are weaning ourselves off of the wares of the world, what do we draw worth from? Where do we place our hopes? What entertains our heart? If it's not movies, television, the web, food, drink, or shopping, I mean.

True fasting is joyful fasting for one primary reason: *it is worship of God.*

One of the reasons we are tempted to let everyone know

we're fasting, to broadcast from the rooftops that we don't have cable or that we only buy from Goodwill, is because we aren't worshiping God so much as the religious admiration of others. False fasting stems even from pleasant hypocrisy and polite self-righteousness; it doesn't have to be "mean" like the Pharisees'. And looking for the strength to fast from others' admiration or approval or even our own good feeling and self-satisfaction over jobs well done will not work out. That well dries up. But a heart tuned to God, drawing strength from him, will have ample supply from which to self-deny. When fasting is an act of worship, practiced as a regular rhythm of life in Christ's kingdom, the Spirit of worship sustains us, a peace that is beyond understanding overcomes us, and a joy unspeakable flows from us.

We do not live in a world where self-denial is encouraged. I have heard maturity defined as "the ability to delay gratification." If this is true, consumer culture is itself immature and is designed to cultivate immaturity. A daily perusal of Twitter and Facebook updates reveals to me the complaints of friends and family (and myself) when the drive-thru line is long, when the lady in front of us at the checkout is digging in her purse for her billfold at the last second, when the airline doesn't serve a meal on a lunchtime flight, when the DVR cuts off the end of our favorite show. In none of these petty irritations over invented problems that don't mean anything in the economy of eternity is there the pure joy found inside the "Enough"-ness of the kingdom.

It is in this world of imaginary problems and required self-service that the cross of Christ is foolishness, because the cross is the very emblem of self-denial, self-emptying, self-sacrifice.

The cross is the polar opposite of wrath displayed over someone taking our parking space. The cross—the place of death and, thereby, life—is the symbol of kingdom fasting, of *joyful fasting*. The author of Hebrews framed it this way:

> Therefore, since we are surrounded by so great a cloud of witnesses, let us also lay aside every weight, and sin which clings so closely, and let us run with endurance the race that is set before us, looking to Jesus, the founder and perfecter of our faith, who for the joy that was set before him endured the cross, despising the shame, and is seated at the right hand of the throne of God. (Heb. 12:1–2)

Jesus endured the cross "for the joy that was set before him." He did not see the sort of gratification in the cross that many of us see in the golden arches or the little green mermaid (or whatever it is Starbucks has in their logo). He saw the gratification of joy beyond the cross, seeing the cross as the means to the gratification of renewed intimacy with the Father ("at the right hand of the throne of God").

You will not be able to say "No, thanks" to everything that belongs to the world if you are not already full as Jesus was filled with the joy of communion with God. And to commune with God is to listen to him. You will find it easier to fast joyfully if you are feasting on the revelation of his Word.

Feasting on the Scriptures and Christ himself prepares us to joyfully fast from the promises of fulfillment made by our consumer culture. When we get the hang of this practice, we walk in yet another kingdom rhythm, the outward effects of life in Christ. This often looks weird.

The rhythm of joyful fasting produces a life of simplicity—intentional, strategic simplicity. Musician and Compassion International advocate Shaun Groves has written many times about joyful fasting. After experiencing the comforts provided by a successful music career and the conveniences of suburban Nashville, Tennessee, Shaun went on a Compassion vision trip to the slums of El Salvador and had his world wrecked. At the end of the trip, before the flight home, the American visitors gathered to share their feelings about their experience. Shaun wrote in his blog:

> When it was my turn to talk about my feelings all I felt was insignificance and so I vomited that emotion up everywhere. (With a lot more words) I said I just didn't care anymore.
>
> About what? About what color we paint the den. About whether my song is climbing the charts. About who the president is. About the gig next week. About what kind of cheese I can get on my Subway sandwich. About seeing that new movie. About that new laptop I wanted. About telling the interviewer what kind of animal I'd like to be. About mowing the yard.
>
> I just didn't care anymore. It didn't feel significant—none of it—not standing back to back with feeding kids, teaching them to read, giving them life-saving medicine, teaching their moms how to sew, telling them they matter to God and to me. Nothing in my whole life back home seemed as significant as my week in El Salvador with Compassion International. Nothing.[4]

Imagining a lifestyle of fasting is sometimes difficult until you actually encounter those who have no choice.

Shaun Groves said "Enough" to "More." He and his family sold their big house and downsized, not because their income decreased or because their family shrank, but simply because they wanted to have more to give away. After that huge first step, they worked diligently to create more simplicity in their life, bringing joyful fasting to bear on more and more areas of their finances and lifestyle.

Do Shaun and millions of others walk in the rhythm of joyful fasting like this to declare how awesome they are? No, they do it because they have tasted the "Enough" in the gospel of the kingdom and because they want others to do so as well. And it is hard to convince others of the goodness of the kingdom of God when we are seen not being able to live without the "goodness" of the world.

Joyful fasting creates a culture of simplicity in our lives and the lives of our churches, enabling us to have the energy, money, and time available to minister the kingdom to others. Joyful fasting empowers us to live out the Beatitudes for those the Beatitudes address.

Here is what God says about this in Isaiah 58:5–7:

> *Is such the fast that I choose,*
> *a day for a person to humble himself?*
> *Is it to bow down his head like a reed,*
> *and to spread sackcloth and ashes under him?*
> *Will you call this a fast,*
> *and a day acceptable to the Lord?*
> *Is not this the fast that I choose:*
> *to loose the bonds of wickedness,*
> *to undo the straps of the yoke,*

to let the oppressed go free,
and to break every yoke?
Is it not to share your bread with the hungry
and bring the homeless poor into your house;
when you see the naked, to cover him,
and not to hide yourself from your own flesh?

Have you heard of the concept of "margin"? Most of us do not have much margin in our lives. We are full to the brim with work, school, bills, church, entertainment, and other obligations and diversions. We don't have much left over for God or others. Many of us don't have much financial margin either. We expand our expenses to the limits of our income, we creep deeper into debt, and we do not save or give much. Yet the simplicity created by joyful fasting provides margin, room to breathe.

Margin also allows us to submit more and more of our living space to the sovereignty of God's Holy Spirit. Remember, the command of God is to love him with our whole selves—all our heart, all our soul, all our mind, all our strength. Jesus didn't tithe his blood, after all. Where do we get off submitting to God only our "religious selves"?

Joyful fasting—faithfully choosing to go without—is how we cede more territory to the Spirit's guidance and comfort. The more we cede, the more we succeed. Paul said not to get drunk with wine (Eph. 5:18), but we could apply his words here to anything. Don't get drunk on busyness, on accomplishments, on congratulations, on social media, on romance, on anything that dilutes your sensitivity to the power of God. Instead, Paul said, "be filled with the Spirit."

The correlation isn't hard to discern: when you are drunk on anything, like wine, it will control you. Your speech, attitude, and behavior will all be influenced by what has intoxicated you. So when you are filled with the Spirit, your speech, attitude, and behavior are heavily influenced by him.

This is the only way to be truly alive.

Fasting Fights Demons

Mark 9 records Jesus' disciples engaged in a violent struggle of spiritual warfare. A boy was sick with demonic possession. The unclean spirit controlling him threw him on the ground, making him lash out frantically and causing him to foam at the mouth. The demon had even tried to kill the boy, prompting him to throw himself into the fire to burn and into water to drown. The disciples weren't able to exorcise this demon, so the boy's father brought him before Jesus, who of course sent the spirit running, never to return.

Later Jesus' disciples asked him why they weren't able to cast the demon out themselves. Jesus replied, "This kind cannot be driven out by anything but prayer" (9:29). Some manuscripts add "and fasting" to that Spiritual recipe for exorcism. In either case or in both, the principle is the same: you don't wield more Spiritual power by adopting extra doses of religion, actualizing more of your inner potential, or naming and claiming more material blessings. You won't see more of the Spirit come to bear through summoning up your own delusions of spiritual grandeur.

You don't have what it takes. It is the very suggestion of the demonic world, in fact, that makes you think that you do. John the Baptist was on the right track, then, when he said, "He must increase, but I must decrease" (John 3:30). John took this seriously, after all, living in animal skins in the desert and living off that now discontinued breakfast cereal, Bugs-n-Honey. What was John doing but intentionally going without in order to supernaturally "go" with God? This is the true purpose of prayer and fasting.

Prayer and fasting put us in closer touch with the weakness in which God's strength is perfected (2 Cor. 12:9). When we are weak, he is strong (v. 10). Prayer and fasting, then, *reduce* us, get more of us out of our way. Prayer and fasting are expressions (and *embracings*) of our weakness and, as such, provide more room for God's strength, which is why prayer and fasting are more effective against devils than all manner of "spiritual" histrionics. The Devil is more afraid of the desperate believer on his face crying out of hunger for the living God than he is of anybody up on his feet rebuking him with random spiritual aphorisms.

The Devil saves pain as a last resort because he knows we are more likely to talk to God when we've run out of earthly comforts. If he can get us sedated with material blessings, drunk on our own worldly consumption, he will "name it and claim it" for us. This is why for most Christians, demonic temptation isn't always explicitly supernatural. Spiritual warfare is more often conducted while we're watching TV or washing our cars in the driveway. Perhaps more spiritual warfare is going on in the comfort of our beds on Sunday morning before church than in the worship services themselves.

Temptation is a part of the fabric of fallen life. Our friend Bill feels tempted to just get by every day, to tune out the still, small voice of the Spirit and listen to all the noise that deludes him.

You and I are tempted by the Devil every time we find ourselves thinking about ourselves too much, dreaming about our lives too much, going about our routines with carelessness too much.

The temptation is subtle, arising very often in a dreadfully contagious disease of the spirit. Ever come down with a case of the *if onlys*? The mom changing her baby's blown-out diaper thinks, *If only I had more help,* or *If only my child was older.* Whatever is challenging her contentment stirs the imagination to want more, better, different.

We think, *If only my spouse was more attentive,* or maybe even, *If only I had a different spouse.* We think if we only had a better job or a better bank account or a better house or a better education or a better family or a better *whatever,* we would finally be happy and satisfied. This is how we say to God, "You are not enough."

This is why contentment and the prayer and fasting that fuel it are radical expressions of Christian belief. The spirit of contentment crushes this demonic self-centeredness.

Intentional fasting from food and anything else provides more space for the Spirit's filling and leading. This is how going without is a blessing. He will fill us; he will satisfy us.

And the more we give up, the more we have to share with others.

You didn't think this was all about you, did you? Well, we'll fix that in our next chapter.

CHAPTER 7

BREAKING FREE FROM THE DRAMA

Experiencing the Spirit's Counsel

Devin is a guy I met once for sushi to talk about his job troubles. We'd never met before, but he was a friend of a friend who asked if I'd get together with him to encourage him. Devin had just moved his family halfway across the country to take a new role at a church. Just a few weeks into this new season, he realized he'd made a terrible mistake.

Really, he'd been bamboozled.

When Devin was interviewing for this role, his prospective employers praised his experience and credentials and affirmed his gifts. They made certain promises related to his place on the team and even regarding his compensation package. Feeling great about the whole prospect and feeling an overwhelming sense of warmth in the invitation, Devin made this big transition.

After arriving, purchasing a new home, and settling in, he had this first surprise: his new employer had promised health insurance, but now that was off the table. But that was just the tip of the iceberg. What ensued over the next few weeks was a gauntlet of relational pain. The leader in charge of the organization began to express doubts about Devin's giftedness and suitability for his role. He'd only been there a few weeks, but where this man had previously talked up Devin's ability, he now brought Devin very low. "I just don't know if you've got what it takes," he said. *Well, okay,* thought Devin, *but that would've been good to know before I moved my family to a new state.*

Over and over again, his boss took seemingly endless opportunities to poke at Devin's sense of security and chip away at his self-confidence. And even when he wasn't aiming his withering doubts at Devin, he was creating a hostile work environment, frequently getting into screaming matches in the hallways with other leaders. Devin felt like he'd entered the Twilight Zone. This man who seemed so sweet, complimentary, and accommodating during the interview process had become a nightmare.

You'd like to think that a ministry environment couldn't abide such toxic leadership, but we all know that many short-tempered narcissists are drawn to church environments, if only because they sense people there are easier to manipulate and bully. This kind of authoritarian leadership is rampant in secular workplaces too. You may have worked for a boss like Devin's. Maybe, heaven forbid, you've been a boss like Devin's.

By the time I met with Devin, he'd already decided he was going to quit. He just didn't know what to do next. He felt burned. Could he walk blindly into another church role? What if it blew up in his face like this one?

Devin's situation may sound unique, but I'm willing to bet you've seen in your own life how past relational hurt makes you reluctant to be vulnerable in the present and future. We all have friends who have endured disastrous romantic relationships and have now "sworn off" dating. We all know ex-pastors who would much rather work the used car lot or sell Amway, since it seems more honest than the last congregation that chewed them up and spit them out. And we all know people for whom every holiday visit becomes more fraught with anxiety than the last, if only because each visit ups the painful ante.

Perhaps it's time to pay another visit to Bill. We last left him as he was assembling a handy list of spiritual life hacks to put more Bible in his life. Ever since his Sunday school classmate Carrie prayed for him, he has felt a bit of the Spirit's unction, an anointing of energy. He has become more regular in his church attendance and more attentive to the words of the songs and the substance of the sermons. He has become more conscious of the messages his environment is trying to feed him daily. He has augmented some of his routine in order to consume more Bible, and while it was a little awkward at first, he is growing accustomed to the routine.

Without thinking in exactly these terms, Bill has decided to submit more of his life to the guidance of the Holy Spirit. He is eradicating noise from his life, mindless busywork from his schedule, and compartmentalization from his spiritual thinking. All of his life belongs to God, he reckons, and all of it ought to be impacted by the gospel. And surprisingly enough, since surrendering more of himself to the Spirit's working, he has never felt freer.

But Bill knows the big test of his "new lease on life" is coming.

Thanksgiving is approaching, and he plans to visit his family in his hometown. This is always difficult for Bill. He struggles not to feel "less than" around his siblings, who are all married and who all make better money and have more exciting jobs. Bill's dad has stopped even trying to figure out what exactly Bill does, and Bill has stopped trying to explain it.

That slight alone would be no big deal. Who cares if your dad doesn't know what you do? But Bill feels keenly the pride his father takes in his other children, how he beams over their (apparently) perfect marriages and brags about their work accomplishments to his friends.

But Bill's dad is not nearly as passive aggressive in his disapproval as Bill's mom. Bill's mom is the queen master of passive aggression. Her martyr complex makes actual martyrs look selfish. According to Bill's mom, he never spends enough time with them when he comes home, never calls home enough, never sends enough cards. You don't have to tell Bill to save the drama for his mama, because his mama displays the most drama of anyone in his life. Bill leaves every family visit emotionally exhausted and feeling utterly defeated.

Maybe you don't have a relational conflict that resembles either Devin's or Bill's. But chances are you can pinpoint some difficulty in your relational life. Maybe it's a hurt from the past you can't quite shake, the haunting memory of someone who never forgave you or whom you yourself have struggled to forgive. Maybe you have a friend or family member who routinely takes advantage of you, and you struggle with the courage to confront them and ask them to repent. Maybe your marriage is broken or your children are prodigals or your best friend is a jerk.

Whoever you are and wherever you are, you're probably not

living much of a relational life if you are not touched in some way by relational conflict. Ever since the fall, our relationships have been a complex web of hurts, fears, worries, and slights.

Would it surprise you to know that the Holy Spirit was sent by God to help with all these kinds of brokenness?

Navigating Broken Relationships Supernaturally

When the Holy Spirit takes up residence in a sinner's heart, he immediately begins renovating the place. It doesn't matter where you placed the furniture before; he's going to rearrange it into a home more suitable for himself. And he's going to start populating the place with new qualities and sharpened attributes. We're going to talk more about the fruit of the Spirit in chapter 8, but here it is enough to say that the Holy Spirit does not bear love, joy, peace, patience, kindness, goodness, faithfulness, gentleness, and self-control (Gal. 5:22–23) *in* us to focus those fruits *on* us. Each of these important character qualities from God's Spirit reach their fullness and most glorify God when they are exemplified in loving service to others. It is great, for instance, if you are generally peaceful. That is a gift from God. But it is better when being peaceful means you are able to forgo vengeance when someone wrongs you. Self-control is great for personal growth and devotion, but self-control hits its apex when it results in margin or abundance with which to share with others in need.

The fruit of the Spirit are the evidences of God's grace fusing into our hearts and minds, conforming our affections and behavioral patterns to the movements of the Spirit and the rhythms of the kingdom. This is something we need gospel power for; we cannot achieve this kind of supernatural outlook on life in and of ourselves. Only the Holy Spirit can establish it in us.

I grew up a very timid, neurotic person. I was easily discouraged and hurt. Consequently it was easy for some people to take advantage of me, to boss me around and manipulate me. Before I had experienced a profound awakening to the gospel of Jesus Christ, I was quite susceptible to passive aggression and bullying. I thought my worth and my identity were always up for grabs, defined by my performance, or at least by others' perception of it.

But something happened to me after I hit rock bottom. I woke up. Or rather, the *Holy Spirit* woke me up. In one moment, on one night according to God's providential design, the Spirit stirred my heart while I was in the midst of some prayerful groanings, burnt up by the bitterness of my sin and broken up by the heavy burden of depression, and he imparted the message of the gospel to my heart in a fresh and exhilarating way. I've never been the same.

I didn't become perfect. No, far from it. But I have a greater and more pronounced sense of Christ's perfection given to me by God's grace. The Holy Spirit had revived me and reminded me of my position with the King and my access to the very throne room itself. I cannot deny this changed the way I responded to all kinds of relational wounds and slights.

As a pastor, I've been subjected to all kinds of passive aggressive manipulation. I've had the biggest donor in my church gently suggest he'd stop giving if I didn't make certain decisions he liked. I've had people try to sabotage me. I've been falsely accused, maliciously maligned, and callously gossiped about. It all hurt, let me tell you. But by God's grace, I was never undone by any of it.

Once you realize the Spirit has hidden you with Christ in God

(Col. 3:3), you realize you don't have anything left to hide. And when you're intentional about awareness of your new identity in Christ (2 Cor. 5:17), you stop feeling like you have something to prove. The Spirit gives you the power to be your true self with both humility and confidence. I call this "gospeling" yourself.

What God graciously does for us is connect us to the eternal reality of his kingdom, which operates on a higher level than the idolatrous kingdoms of this world. Believing in the gospel of the kingdom tunes our hearts to heaven and its frequency. This may sound weird, but when we walk in step with the Spirit, it is like inhabiting another dimension even while participating in the regular world.

When Bill sets his heart on grace and prepares to "gospel" his heart out of any hurts or confusion he may be tempted to wallow in at Thanksgiving, he is in a very real sense operating in a completely different dimension than his parents and siblings. The digs and barbs come, but he's like Neo in *The Matrix*, dodging all those bullets as if in slow motion. The Spirit has bent reality for him, helping him to see that whatever hurtful or discouraging things are said to or about him aren't the final and true words— not about him, not about his life, and not even about reality.

This may sound like pretending, but it's really the other way around. Whenever we hurt someone, whether intentionally or by neglect, we are operating according to the perversion of God's created order. His original design for men and women was to know him fully and joyfully and, consequently, through him to know each other. Husbands and wives, by the Spirit, are meant to experience unashamed nakedness with one another. Every human being, by the Spirit, is meant to love his neighbor as himself.

But the cosmic treason of sin has divorced us from God and consequently has divorced us from one another. And yet, through the gospel of Jesus Christ, God's Spirit is still on the scene, still wooing people back into fellowship with others, still reconstructing what we've broken and mending what we've torn. Look at how Paul connected relational health to moving in accordance with the Spirit:

> Therefore, having put away falsehood, let each one of you speak the truth with his neighbor, for we are members one of another. Be angry and do not sin; do not let the sun go down on your anger, and give no opportunity to the devil. Let the thief no longer steal, but rather let him labor, doing honest work with his own hands, so that he may have something to share with anyone in need. Let no corrupting talk come out of your mouths, but only such as is good for building up, as fits the occasion, that it may give grace to those who hear. And do not grieve the Holy Spirit of God, by whom you were sealed for the day of redemption. Let all bitterness and wrath and anger and clamor and slander be put away from you, along with all malice. Be kind to one another, tenderhearted, forgiving one another, as God in Christ forgave you. (Eph. 4:25–32)

What did Paul mean in verse 30 when he referred to the grieving of the Spirit? In context, he was making an inextricable connection between walking by the Spirit and interpersonal wholeness. When we lie about others, give in to anger and unforgiveness, adopt a posture of stinginess, curse others, grow bitter, cultivate wrath, and engage in slander, we grieve the Spirit because we've stopped walking in his footsteps. We grieve the

Spirit by resisting his impact on the way we live our lives, even if simply going on spiritual "autopilot," because that means we are susceptible to the shaping values of the world and the temptations of the Devil.

On the other hand, when we put all those things away and instead treat others with kindness, tenderness, and forgiveness, we commend the Spirit's work in our lives. And the wonderful thing is, when we consciously and conscientiously submit ourselves to the Spirit's work, he seeds and grows more and more kindness, tenderness, and forgiveness within us.

Christians have the power to "do relationships" in an entirely unworldly way. If we will set our minds on things above and remember that we are not our own, we will become fertile ground for relational transformation. The Spirit does this because his aim is to glorify the Son and proclaim the gospel, and these aims cannot be accomplished if we aren't loving others, including— especially?—the people who hurt us.

The primary means by which we get out of our own relational way is repenting of our aspirations to godhood.

Repenting of Confirmation-Bias Christianity

Have you ever heard of confirmation bias? Confirmation bias is the tendency to interpret new evidence as confirmation of one's existing beliefs or theories.

You and I see this every day in the world of social media, and it gets ramped up, for instance, over every election cycle. When it comes to political pontificating, my Facebook feed in particular appears to be one huge exercise in confirmation bias—my liberal friends share and "amen" articles, videos, and memes that fit their preadopted left-leaning narratives, and my conservative friends share and "amen" articles, videos, and memes that fit their preadopted right-leaning ones.

I've been guilty of this myself. It is stunningly easy to fall into this confirmation bias thing. If something sounds true—meaning, it seems to fit what we already believe—we believe it to be true without corroboration. It is the widespread epidemic of confirmation bias that has given us the relatively new phenomenon known as "fake news."

But there's a spiritual component at play here too. The reason we fall into confirmation bias politically is not essentially a political problem. It is a human problem, which is to say, it is a sin problem—which is to say, it is a problem of self-interest and self-worship. The truth is, you and I are prone to conducting our entire lives along the narratives constructed from confirmation bias.

What is our bias?

Put simply, we think that we are the center of the universe. That our happiness is what is most important in life and that our preferences are—or ought to be—the laws of the land.

"Man's nature, so to speak, is a perpetual factory of idols," John Calvin once said.[1] We are never *not* worshiping. But there is one big idol that all our little manufactured idols themselves serve, and that idol is us. There's really no new idolatry in our brave new world; we just find new ways with which to orient our worlds around ourselves. So whatever fits this bias is deemed "true." And whatever does not is repudiated or simply ignored.

How would you know if your Christian life has become hijacked by confirmation bias? Here are some possible diagnostic signs:

- When you hear a particularly challenging or convicting sermon, you think mainly of who else needs to hear it or who else it ought to apply to—*I really hope my spouse/child/friend/etc., is listening right now*—instead of how it might apply personally to you.
- You don't really have close friends who know the struggles going on in your private world—your family, your marriage, your workplace, etc.
- You don't pray much for God's forgiveness.
- You think every strained or broken relationship you've ever experienced has always been the other person's fault and you struggle to see how you might have contributed to the problem.
- You have a problem with your temper.
- You constantly rehearse the failings of others in your mind and imagine dialogues with them in which you "put them in their place" and "win."
- You passive-aggressively say things aloud or share things on social media that you mean for other people to be chastened or convicted by.
- You have a ready stack of excuses for your problems and sins but not many for others, especially those who've offended you in some way.
- You inwardly enjoy it when someone you dislike fails in some way.
- If you say, "I'm sorry," it is often followed by the word *if*, and if you say, "I forgive you," it is often followed by the word *but*.
- You have a tendency to say, "I told you so."

If more than one of those signs fit you, you may be a confirmation-bias Christian.

So, you may be wondering, what's the antidote? How do we Spiritually work against our confirmation bias?

1. Examine Yourself

Knowing and acknowledging we have a confirmation-bias problem is necessary before we can even address it. The problem with confirmation bias is that our biases are embedded, they are presumed, felt as "natural." So we aren't typically conscious that we're doing these things. Paul told Timothy to "keep a close watch on yourself" (1 Tim. 4:16).

2. Repent

Jesus said that if people wanted to come after him, they must deny themselves and take up their crosses. Therefore we must be constantly repenting and thus constantly redirecting our bias outward, away from ourselves, and constantly redirecting our indictments inward, into our own souls. Martin Luther said, "All of life is repentance,"[2] because, as Jesus said, this taking up of our crosses must happen daily and because every day we wake up biased toward ourselves and against others.

3. Press the Gospel "Reset" Every Day

Remember that Christ's mercies for us are new every morning. And this mercy is meant to be shared, not hoarded. When we remind ourselves of our union with Christ, we cultivate a fearlessness to repent, a boldness to "own up," a courage to be transparent with others, and an impulse to love our neighbors as much as we love ourselves.

Receiving from the Spirit What You Want from Others

So there is Bill at Thanksgiving. Just as he expected, he is wrestling with envy and bitterness about the allegedly better lives of his siblings. He knows that treating them unkindly based purely on his own emotions and nothing that they've ever done or said to him is petty and immature. Because he has become more and more satisfied by the Holy Spirit through his newly adopted daily disciplines, he is not simply conscious of this weakness, but he finds the strength to actually enjoy his siblings' presence. He is happy that they are happy. He is glad that they are thankful for healthy families and a relatively trouble-free year, and he is thankful for them. He doesn't feel "less than" in their presence at the dinner table because he's already been feasting on the Good News with his King.

But then there's Bill's dad. Once again he saves his glowing words and big smiles for Bill's siblings. But Bill begins to empathize. He knows his dad isn't trying to slight him. He's simply not aware. And remarkably Bill begins to find it pleasing that his dad would be so happy on Thanksgiving Day, surrounded by all his children and grandchildren. Bill realizes that his biggest problem with his dad is himself and his own need to be the center of attention.

I spoke at a conference once on the subject of God's amazing love for us and the freedom that his love gives us to walk humbly and confidently amid the difficulties of life. After I had spoken, a young man approached me with tears in his eyes. He said that he knew that God loved him, but he struggled to feel it because he didn't believe anyone else did.

What was this man's problem? It is something you and I have faced throughout our lives in different ways. The gospel he heard intellectually he was not feeling experientially. Or, as I once heard Tim Keller put it, the gospel was on audio but the law was on video. He was aware intellectually of God's grace (audio), but the world he lived in seemed steeped in a climate of measurement and merit.

I asked that young man a few questions about his life and relationships to discern if perhaps he was in an abusive situation of some kind, physical or otherwise, that was more deeply problematic. He shared that mainly he just didn't feel like he belonged anywhere. I have felt that way, too, and in fact, it was something personal I had shared in my message that had prompted him to approach me.

He said that when he lived at home, he was immersed in a particular ethnic culture that dealt largely in shame. Relationships were inauthentic and superficial in his family and church because nobody felt the freedom to open themselves up to criticism or to stand out from the crowd. Achievement and accomplishment were the currency of his culture, and anyone who fell short was treated as a failure. This kind of pressure coupled with the pronounced lack of affection and encouragement had taken their toll on his psyche.

Then he left home for school, and while he hoped things would be different in a new environment, he found himself alienated once again. An intellectual and theological sort, he considered most of his peers disinterested in deep discussions and thoughtful debates. Nobody read very many books that weren't assigned for classes. Nobody seemed too concerned about the deep things of God.

For this young man, who never had someone close enough to be his "me too" kind of friend, his life thus far had been one marked by solitude and grief. He had left one kind of loneliness and entered another.

Understanding this personal similarity, in that moment, I followed the Spirit's prompting away from whatever grievance he might have with certain people or whatever sense of not being included he felt at his school and suggested that he work at reorienting his perspective. "Is it possible," I asked him, "that you enter into every potential relationship wondering how that person might satisfy your need for companionship and solve your need to be loved?"

He agreed that that wasn't just possible; he was most definitely doing that. In fact, that was one thing that was beginning to bother him. He now felt that his alienation was beginning to have less to do with his not "fitting in" and more to do with his always *needing* to feel like he fit in. Without trying, influenced by his loneliness, he had become the relational sponge in small groups, the hangdog sad sack at fellowships, the "Debbie Downer" among what friends he still had left.

This young man's felt needs became his relational operating system, which meant he had begun treating others as though they existed primarily to show him love. So this had become a self-perpetuating cycle. If the primary way you relate to others is to get love from them, you will always be dissatisfied, because nobody can love you like God can. Biblical counselor and author Edward T. Welch calls this dynamic "when people are big and God is small."[3]

If anything, awakening to this relational propensity for self-centeredness should have made this guy feel less alone, since nearly every single person since the fall of humankind has fallen prey to this self-centered way of doing relationships. We seek in others what we can find only in God. Consequently, we never quite feel loved and the people we want love from, over time, end up feeling used.

Our illustrative friend Bill has not fully wrapped his mind around this reality yet, but he is beginning to experience the shifting dynamic all the same. Having become more and more regularly filled by the Spirit through engaging in the divine dynamic of friendship with God, he finds himself less needy at Thanksgiving dinner. He discovers that while he used to be racked with guilt and envy and woundedness in that situation, now his inner life seems much more tranquil. This is what pastor Jeff Vanderstelt said about handling relationally complex situations: "Quiet your soul and listen to God. And close your mouth once in a while and listen to others. Do both together, and you will find yourself joining in with the activity of the Spirit working through you as his dwelling place."[4]

Christians want to be channels of the Spirit's working in the world. We can't do that, however, if we're constantly worried about having our needs met by others. When we realize that our cup has been filled already by the Holy Spirit working through the gospel of Jesus, we begin to see ourselves more as need-meeters than need-takers.

Of course, no amount of Spiritual perspective makes the wrongs people do to us right or the hurtful things they say to us "okay." But following the Spirit's counsel through these complex interactions can affect how we interpret, process, and respond. Keeping our ear close to the Spirit's application of the Scriptures in our heart, in fact, is how we end up (super)naturally loving our enemies and blessing those who persecute us.

What We Owe Others

If the Great Commandment is to love God with everything we have and then to love our neighbors at least as much as we love ourselves, the vast majority of us have a lot of repenting to do.

The American church has done a great disservice in merging one's journey of faith with the values of the American dream. We like to use phrases like "personal Lord and Savior" and "personal relationship with Jesus," neither of which is wrong, per se, but neither do they reflect the fullness of life in Jesus' kingdom. The truth is that while we are saved as individuals, we are not saved to an individual walk. And while our faith may be personal, it is not private. Christianity is not meant to occupy one time slot in the weekly programming of our life.

After he had murdered Abel, Cain was called out by God about his brother's whereabouts. Cain responded defensively, dismissively: "Am I my brother's keeper?" (Gen. 4:9 NIV). Many of us every day basically ask with our lives, "Am I my brother's keeper?"

And as much as we answer with an implied "No" with our lives, the answer is unequivocally "Yes"—*if* you mean to abide in Christ in the glory of his kingdom. Some of us live as though all we need to do is not commit some gross sin, or at least not commit a sin that is grosser than anybody else's. But personal morality is not the point of the kingdom either. Take a look at this revelation about the destruction of Sodom and Gomorrah: "Behold, this was the guilt of your sister Sodom: she and her daughters had pride, excess of food, and prosperous ease, but did not aid the poor and needy" (Ezek. 16:49).

Despite all the sexual immorality and violence in Sodom, the sin God focuses on here is the selfish neglect of the poor and needy by those who were comfortable and content. Does this sound like anybody you know?

In consumer culture, faith just becomes another add-on, customized and personalized for our own needs and tastes. We see this in everything from church programming to Christian product marketing. We see it in the proof of our lives, which keeps us on a track of self-tailored spirituality yet barren in the fruit of the Spirit.

But faith in Christ, despite being an inward conviction, has outward manifestation, particularly in the grace-driven connecting to other people. If our faith is just an inward experience, it is fundamentally a self-help project. In such inward faith, Jesus is Dr. Phil or Dr. Drew, not the Lord of the universe or the bridegroom of the church.

Consider the following Scriptures:

"In the same way, let your light shine before others, so that they may see your good works and give glory to your Father who is in heaven." (Matt. 5:16)

For we are his workmanship, created in Christ Jesus for good works, which God prepared beforehand, that we should walk in them. (Eph. 2:10)

As each has received a gift, use it to serve one another, as good stewards of God's varied grace. (1 Peter 4:10)

If our citizenship is first and foremost in the world we live in, it makes very good sense to devote our allegiance to ourselves.

We do live in a democracy, after all (or at least, a representative republic). The power lies with the people, and our birthright is life, liberty, and the pursuit of happiness. But if my citizenship is first and foremost in the kingdom and my heart has become a throne for King Jesus, all bets are off.

In John 3:3 Jesus blew the mind of a Pharisee named Nicodemus by saying, "Truly, truly, I say to you, unless one is born again he cannot see the kingdom of God." The whole concept of being "born again" speaks to the resurrection-quality life Jesus brings in and through himself. Basically Jesus is saying that to experience the kingdom, we have to be made alive for the first time—again! The whole notion of being born again speaks to new life, new identity, new status, new *everything*. Included in this everything is a new citizenship and its accompanying new allegiance.

Paul said that "our citizenship is in heaven" (Phil. 3:20). We abide in the kingdom while the kingdom is distinct from the world. We live and speak as if Jesus is the ruler over us, as if the gospel is our law, as if the church is our community, and as if the kingdom's permanence outweighs the temporary concerns of the world. It's not just citizenship that changes when we are born again, but our allegiance.

The allegiance of those born again is to Jesus, but in and through Jesus also to our neighbor. This is the point of parables like the good Samaritan and commands like the Great Commandment. Jesus makes care for others nonnegotiable for kingdom living. John put it this way: "We know that we have passed out of death into life, because we love the brothers. Whoever does not love abides in death" (1 John 3:14).

The litmus test for whether one has been born again is love

for others. This principle is set up by Jesus himself in John 13:35, when he says, "By this all people will know that you are my disciples, if you have love for one another."

The connection between love for God and love for others is inextricable. According to the Bible, it doesn't even make sense to say we love God but don't love others. Peter learned in John 21 that to love Jesus is to feed his sheep. To love God truly is to love others. Jesus solidifies this truth in the Great Commandment: "'You shall love the Lord your God with all your heart and with all your soul and with all your strength and with all your mind, and your neighbor as yourself'" (Luke 10:27).

In Christ's mind, there is not just duplicity in love for God and neglect of neighbor, but there is death as well. This startling reality will come crashing home for many in the judgment:

> "Then he will say to those on his left, 'Depart from me, you cursed, into the eternal fire prepared for the devil and his angels. For I was hungry and you gave me no food, I was thirsty and you gave me no drink, I was a stranger and you did not welcome me, naked and you did not clothe me, sick and in prison and you did not visit me.' Then they also will answer, saying, 'Lord, when did we see you hungry or thirsty or a stranger or naked or sick or in prison, and did not minister to you?' Then he will answer them, saying, 'Truly, I say to you, as you did not do it to one of the least of these, you did not do it to me.'" (Matt. 25:41–45)

We aren't just ignoring nameless, faceless, needy people every day. We are ignoring, neglecting, scorning, and shaming Jesus. It is Jesus we pass by every day while we are on our track, gazing downward, preoccupied with self and its interests.

In a very real spiritual sense, then, to abide in Christ means to abide in our neighbors. Certainly in a physical sense, to abide with Christ means to abide in the presence of our neighbors, to care for and comfort them, to love them at the very least as much as we love ourselves. When we approach our faith as consumers, we keep Jesus at a distance and consequently others as well. But when we get closer to Jesus, we get closer to others drawn to him and to those to whom he leads us.

The good news is that being born again empowers and equips us to love others; the rhythms of the kingdom include this rhythm of service and generosity, and this rhythm is something the Holy Spirit produces in and through you.

Back to Bill at Thanksgiving. Now Bill does not see his mom as a necessary meeter of his emotional needs. He also begins to see himself in relation to Jesus as she is in relation to him. How many times has he slighted Jesus, hurt Jesus, ignored Jesus, failed to honor Jesus? And yet Jesus continues to love him and receive him, overlooking faults and forgiving sins. Maybe with Jesus' help, he can extend that same kind of love to his mother.

Bill discovers that even as he *thinks* about embracing this posture, he feels a bit of Spiritual power helping him along.

The Blessed Emptiness

The formula is simple: we are able to love only because God first loved us. First John 4:19 says so.

The formula for relational self-crucifixion runs parallel: Jesus gave his life as a ransom for many, so we are to give our lives to others as well. We see ourselves as need-meeters rather than need-takers. Jesus has given us his life, so we are set free to give up our own for others.

The Spirit's counsel to our inner life, then, creates a heart beating with generosity, a posture of sacrifice, and a vision of compassion in the world. It means repenting of relational legalism—where we treat others based only on what they can do for us—and the exploitation of the weak, the ignoring of our neighbor, the neglect of others. It means repenting of not noticing!

Paul found the joy in this humble servitude, this sacrificial service: "Even if I am to be poured out as a drink offering upon the sacrificial offering of your faith, I am glad and rejoice with you all" (Phil. 2:17).

The image of being "poured out" is powerful. It reflects emptying. It holds up the poured-out life of Christ at the cross as the central motivation for service to others. We are constantly filling ourselves up with all sorts of things, typically things not very good for us.

When we are full from the Spiritual provisions found in our daily friendship with God, we can then make room in our life by fasting. And when we have the resources of Scripture and intimacy with God and the freedom of fasting, we are now able to give and serve with joy. These are all the rhythms Jesus practiced in order to present himself as a worthy sacrifice for the debt of sin.

Lift up your eyes and see that Jesus has stooped down low to us.

Earlier in Philippians 2, Paul set up the gospel of Christ's self-emptying and humility: "Have this mind among yourselves, which is yours in Christ Jesus, who, though he was in the form of

God, did not count equality with God a thing to be grasped, but emptied himself, by taking the form of a servant, being born in the likeness of men" (vv. 5–7).

This beautiful proclamation of the blessed emptiness of Jesus Christ is what makes our service possible and powerful. What an amazing God we have that he takes the route of subservience and sacrificial death to best establish the sovereignty and supremacy of his Son! This can only mean that our service and sacrifice are what will demonstrate that Christ—not us—is sovereign over our lives and that Christ—not us—is supreme in our lives.

All of this beautiful emptying is preparing us for a beautiful filling. And all of our blessed deconstruction of self-idolatry and self-importance is preparing us for a blessed construction. The Holy Spirit is not creating supernatural lone rangers. He is doing something through our redeemed relationships that in our narrow individualistic vision we would never have conceived of ourselves. The Holy Spirit is making a church.

The Unbabeling of Babel

Larry Norman, late pioneer of Christian rock, once sang, "Everybody has to choose whether they will win or lose, follow God or sing the blues, and who they're gonna sin with."[5] I've always thought that was pretty clever. Because when you get right down to it, we are all making that choice.

Sometimes you hear people say they don't go to church because it's full of hypocrites. This is definitely true. But it's not like the outside world is some kind of hypocrisy-free zone. Maybe you do see the same kinds of sins among Christians as you do among non-Christians, and this is a painful reality that the New Testament is neither ignorant of nor ambivalent about. And yet one thing the church has going for it is that (most of) the people who align themselves with it acknowledge they are sinners!

This is what I take Larry Norman to mean—not that we ought to choose some people with whom to engage willingly in sin, but that we're all sinners and we're going to fail and engage in relational messiness, so why not align with other people who realize that and are seeking help from Jesus? If I have no choice but to pick a culture to "sin with," I'm going to pick the one that is warring with that sin, holding me accountable for that sin—perhaps even disciplining me for it—and constantly pointing me to the Jesus who forgives my sin, taking it to the cross to kill it. We all have to choose who we're going to sin with. Why not choose the church?

If we could understand just what is taking place Spiritually in and through the messy fellowship of repenting sinners seeking help from God through Christ, we wouldn't be so reluctant to immerse ourselves in relationships with them. What prevents us from doing so, no matter our stated reasons, is the spirit of Babel.

Do you remember the story of the Tower of Babel? The people of earth sought to build a tower reaching all the way to heaven (Gen. 11:1–9). They were blatant about their reasons for doing so: to "make a name for ourselves" (11:4). They were also concerned about dispersion, so in a way, they were trying to experience community. But it was not the kind of community God had mandated for them. This attempt at community was one built on self-interest and human glory. If you know the story, you know what happened next. "So the LORD dispersed them from there over the face of all the earth, and they left off building the city. Therefore its name was called Babel, because there the LORD confused the language of all the earth" (11:8–9).

This is not an account of the entrance of sin into the world—that happened at the fall of humankind when Adam disobeyed. But this ancient disaster was another great explanation for why our attempts at relationships and fellowship are so fraught with difficulty. We are, in effect, speaking different languages. I am trying to do relationships in a way that satisfies me; you are trying to do relationships in a way that satisfies you. We're not on the same page, and we both think we're going to lose if the other doesn't get on our page.

This relational chaos became part of the communal DNA throughout the history that ensued. God's people could never quite get it together. They turned on each other, and they became way too comfortable with the idolatry of the surrounding nations. But when we fast-forward to the earthly ministry of Jesus and its aftereffects, we see something astounding. What God had torn apart, he was beginning to put together.

Before Jesus' death and resurrection, he told his followers that he was going to "go away" so that he could send the Helper to them. And after he ascended to heaven, he made good on his promise. The Holy Spirit officially descended upon the earth, and he did so in dramatic fashion.

> When the day of Pentecost arrived, they were all together in one place. And suddenly there came from heaven a sound like a mighty rushing wind, and it filled the entire house where they were sitting. And divided tongues as of fire appeared to them

and rested on each one of them. And they were all filled with the Holy Spirit and began to speak in other tongues as the Spirit gave them utterance.

Now there were dwelling in Jerusalem Jews, devout men from every nation under heaven. And at this sound the multitude came together, and they were bewildered, because each one was hearing them speak in his own language. And they were amazed and astonished, saying, "Are not all these who are speaking Galileans? And how is it that we hear, each of us in his own native language? Parthians and Medes and Elamites and residents of Mesopotamia, Judea and Cappadocia, Pontus and Asia, Phrygia and Pamphylia, Egypt and the parts of Libya belonging to Cyrene, and visitors from Rome, both Jews and proselytes, Cretans and Arabians—we hear them telling in our own tongues the mighty works of God." And all were amazed and perplexed, saying to one another, "What does this mean?" (Acts 2:1–12)

It means that the Spirit was knitting back together by grace what had become unraveled by sin. Pentecost was the unbabeling of Babel.

Through the Spirit's unifying work, sinners can finally get on the same page because the Spirit is helping us to deny ourselves, take up our crosses, and follow Jesus. And when we all have our sights set on Jesus, we stop thinking about our own glory and begin basking in his.

This new community reknit together by the Spirit's power is a new humanity, a new civilization, a new culture running counter to the competing cultures of the world. And while this new community is made up of the same kinds of sinners you find in other places, it is nevertheless the only community that will prevail against the gates of hell (Matt. 16:18).

When you choose to sin with the world, you go the way the world is going. But when you choose to join the sinner-saints in the body of Christ, the same people you sin with are the people you'll reign with. If you are going to spend eternity with these people, you should probably start figuring out how to live with them now. This is the whole point of human relationships, really—to glorify God by living graciously with others as Christ has lived graciously with us. When you think about it that way, taking the risk of engaging relationships in the church is no risk at all. And yet it's startling how many people try to do Christian life apart from church.

Bill was doing that. Oh sure, he was attending a weekly church service. But he wasn't really engaged. He was checking something off the duty list crafted for the religious side of himself. He saw church as a thing to be used, a resource for his own personal development. Until he followed the Spirit's conviction about the emptiness of his life and went a little deeper, he hadn't considered the deep well of grace that might even be found among weak people huddling around Jesus together.

A few years ago I wrote a book called *Gospel Wakefulness* about the profound experience of grace many Christians go through that takes them into an almost hyperdrive in their sanctification. Someone recently suggested that a good follow-up to that theme might be *Local Church Wakefulness*, since evangelicalism in the West is so beset by professing Christians who don't think of themselves as obligated to or even relationally immersed in a local church.

The church is where God's Spirit is doing the grand rebuilding of humanity and human relationships. To consider the church optional is to miss out on the fullness of the Holy Spirit's super-naturalizing of humankind!

Further, to withhold ourselves from the life of a local church is to abandon the very mission of God in the world to advance Christ's kingdom through the spreading of the gospel. If you want to participate in the truly supernatural life in this earthly world, you will follow the Spirit's call first into the church, since, as one theologian says, "The church is an agent of the Spirit."[6] Therefore, to ignore the church is to quench the Spirit.

Of course, all of this is easier said than done. Bill may walk out of that Thanksgiving dinner still feeling a little beat up. Adopting the wimpy posture of a human doormat comes easily. But this is not the same thing as choosing to love. Bill may leave his holiday at home weary from the spiritual warfare against his own flesh, but he can also walk out victorious because he realizes the security the Spirit has given him through the blossoming fruit of patience, peace, and gentleness. And Bill can keep going deeper at his local church, not simply attending Sunday school to participate in discussions but seeking out more regular fellowship in small groups, formal and informal. He has tasted and seen that the Spirit's work is real and powerful, and now he wants more.

Some wounds go deeper than mere relational conflict, however. We all know what it's like to deal with difficult people. Jesus' words on taking up our crosses certainly have some application for that scenario, but surely they mean more than merely putting up with an annoying coworker or passive-aggressive family member. When Jesus told his first-century followers to take up their crosses, they immediately thought of death. And this word must have resonance for those moments when what we feel is more like a death.

Some wounds, relational or not, go much deeper than "hurt feelings." Some dark clouds aren't easily dismissed. Some afflictions persist until it would seem hope is nothing more than a fairy tale. What does it look like to live supernaturally when the natural world is killing us?

CHAPTER 8

HOLDING ON TO HOPE WHEN THE DAYS ARE DARK

Experiencing the Spirit's Comfort

One of the most startlingly supernatural moments in the New Testament's account of the early church is the conversion of Saul of Tarsus. From beginning to end, this man's life endured a radical Spiritual makeover no natural means could orchestrate.

Saul was an infamous persecutor of Christians, a murderer. He was as relentless and ruthless as he was religious, which was very. Saul was not seeking God; in fact, he believed firmly that he had already found him. And he was convinced, beyond a shadow of a doubt, that snuffing out followers of Jesus was what God wanted him to do. So saying that God interrupted Saul "out of the blue" would not be hyperbole. Indeed, it was a blazing revelation of Christ's glory in the sky that began to change everything for Saul.

Acts 9 recounts the fateful day Saul got hijacked by the gospel. He was on his way to Damascus to kill more Christians, but God had other plans: "Now as he went on his way, he approached Damascus, and suddenly a light from heaven shone around him. And falling to the ground, he heard a voice saying to him, 'Saul, Saul, why are you persecuting me?' And he said, 'Who are you, Lord?' And he said, 'I am Jesus, whom you are persecuting'" (vv. 3–5).

Saul was left utterly undone by this encounter. The revelation left him blind for three days, and he was unable to eat or drink anything. Reflecting on his conversion in one of his letters, Saul—later called Paul—described the experience as being "owned," or, in some translations, "laid hold of" or "apprehended" (Phil. 3:12). Paul was waylaid by Jesus.

So miraculous was Paul's turnaround that the greatest earthly accuser the church had known now became perhaps the church's greatest earthly advocate. Paul was now not only willing to give up killing believers, he was willing to be killed with them. And where he once occupied a position of privilege and power, he now gladly accepted persecution for Christ.

He didn't have to wait for long. Acts 9, which begins with Paul's conversion, relates first his rocky entrance into the body of Christ—because how would you respond if the guy trying to kill you suddenly announced he was on your team?—and then his dangerous assumption of the apostolic ministry for which he would later be martyred. In verse 23 we read that the Jews want to kill him. In verse 29 we read that the Greeks want to kill him.

Let's not gloss over this. It's easy to read this casually two thousand years after the fact from the comfort of our couch or coffee shop. What would it be like if, everywhere you went, people wanted to murder you? How would that affect your thought processes? How would it affect your behavior? How would it affect your theology?

This was just the beginning for Paul. Later he ran down the laundry list of sufferings he had accepted as part of his missionary life:

> Are they servants of Christ? I am a better one—I am talking like a madman—with far greater labors, far more imprisonments, with countless beatings, and often near death. Five times I received at the hands of the Jews the forty lashes less one. Three times I was beaten with rods. Once I was stoned. Three times I was shipwrecked; a night and a day I was adrift at sea; on frequent journeys, in danger from rivers, danger from robbers, danger from my own people, danger from Gentiles, danger in the city, danger in the wilderness, danger at sea, danger from false brothers; in toil and hardship, through many a sleepless night, in hunger and thirst, often without food, in cold and exposure. And, apart from other things, there is the daily pressure on me of my anxiety for all the churches. (2 Cor. 11:23–28)

If anyone ever knew suffering, it was Paul. This man regularly enjoyed the Spiritual anointing touted by so many we see on TV while experiencing none of their opulent comforts. And yet Paul—like Job—discovered something otherworldly through all this experience. He discovered that to really live, we must really die. And he learned that the darkness so many of us endure is often meant to make the glory of Christ shine more brightly.

There in the middle of Acts 9, between the anxiety of the church over Paul and the anxiety of Paul over his would-be assassins, we find this amazing little verse: "So the church throughout all Judea and Galilee and Samaria had peace and was being built up. And walking in the fear of the Lord and in the comfort of the Holy Spirit, it multiplied" (9:31). Amid our depression, doubt, discouragement, and even death, we can have peace. The Holy Spirit will comfort us and help us, just as Jesus said he would.

When You're Making More Sounds Than Words

As we've learned previously, it is when we are at our weakest that the strength of the Lord shines best. Jesus is specifically looking for the poor in spirit to bless them with the riches of his grace. Since this is true, it stands to reason that the poorer our spirit becomes, the more of his riches we can realize. This is especially comforting to know when you are at the end of your rope.

I'm not talking about having a bad day. I'm talking more about having a bad *life*. Some of you reading this book can see no end to your pain. You can see no real way out. You may or may not believe Jesus Christ has wonderful plans for you, but you've likely come to suspect he means after this life is over.

Some of you are dealing with tremendous pain that words cannot even adequately describe. Even telling your "story" to friends or to your small group or to your therapist seems to fall short of adequately expressing the pain you feel.

I am grateful for the realism of the Bible on the human condition. Romans 8 is one of my favorite passages of Scripture.

It is a masterpiece within the masterpiece of Paul's epistle. I love its declarations of assurance, security, and victory. And I love the way it accurately captures what it's like to feel pain beyond words. Capturing just how pervasively painful we feel, Paul said that the sin and brokenness of the fall is felt both personally and cosmically: "And not only the creation, but we ourselves, who have the firstfruits of the Spirit, groan inwardly as we wait eagerly for adoption as sons, the redemption of our bodies" (Rom. 8:23). We are dying, and we know it. We feel it. Our frailty causes us to groan.

But three verses later he mentioned something curious. We don't groan alone: "Likewise the Spirit helps us in our weakness. For we do not know what to pray for as we ought, but the Spirit himself intercedes for us with groanings too deep for words" (8:26).

What can this mean?

Well, surely you know what it is like yourself to groan. Maybe you've been in a situation so painful, so apparently hopeless, that even your prayers are more noises than words. I can vividly remember that dark season in my own life. I recall offering up nothing but my incoherent sobs as prayer offerings to God. He could certainly translate the cries of my heart. My groanings were too deep for English words.

You probably know what that's like. But did you know the Spirit does that *with you*?

In his remarkably helpful little book on Romans 8, Ray Ortlund commented on the complementary truths of Romans 8:23 and 8:26: "In verse 23, we groan. In verse 26, the Spirit groans—through our own struggles in prayer. He is *in* our struggles, directing our faith to God, not letting our faith die, helping our hope to persevere. He is lifting, through our wordless yearnings, prayers that he himself translates into the wisdom of heaven."[1]

Yes, the Holy Spirit is in our struggles. He's there. There's no cavern so dark that the omnipresent Spirit isn't there. There's no hole so deep that the omnipotent Spirit's power isn't deeper still. There is no depression so dreadful that the omniscient Spirit isn't speaking. In fact, it's in these depths that we see just how deep God's grace sinks.

And to know more of God's grace is a good thing! This is the bittersweet irony of Christian suffering. It is why Paul, after all he had been through and had yet to go through, could speak of suffering as if it were a privilege (Phil. 1:29). It's why he could call suffering a "light momentary affliction" (2 Cor. 4:17).

One of the best modern books I've recently read on the Spirit's comfort in suffering is Wesley Hill's *Washed and Waiting*, in which Hill masterfully reflected on the often excruciating life of taking up one's cross as a Christian warring against same-sex attraction. Where the natural thinking of the world would insist Hill give up his "religious superstition" and embrace "who he really is," he chose celibacy, trusting that in the end, the Lord would use his struggle to sanctify him. Hill wrote:

> One of the hardest-to-swallow, most countercultural, counter-intuitive implications of the gospel is that bearing up under a difficult burden with patient perseverance is a *good* thing. The gospel actually advocates this kind of endurance as a daily "dying" for and with Jesus. While those in the grip of Christ's love will never experience ultimate defeat, there is a profound

sense in which we must face our struggles now knowing there may be no real relief this side of God's new creation.[2]

This is a difficult realization to accept, but the truth is, the Lord is always more interested in deepening our sense of need for him than he is in giving us reasons not to need him at all. This is especially true of our deepest longings and biggest struggles. Hill went on to say:

> This kind of long-suffering endurance is not a special assignment the gospel only gives to gay and lesbian persons. Many believers of all stripes and backgrounds struggle with desires of various sorts that they must deny in order to remain faithful to the gospel's demands. Homosexual Christians who choose to remain celibate "must face the dilemma of a life without sexual fulfillment," wrote Francis Schaeffer in a letter to a friend. "We may cry with them concerning this, but we must not let the self-pity get too deep, because the unmarried girl who has strong sexual desires, and no one asks her to marry, has the same problem. In both cases this is surely a part of the abnormality of the fallen world." Schaeffer's language and outlook may be a bit old-fashioned, but his point is entirely in keeping with the spirit of the gospel.[3]

Yes, Schaeffer's point is entirely in keeping with the spirit of the gospel, and this is why it applies to you, too, whatever your situation. Maybe you struggle with same-sex attraction. Or maybe your struggle is entirely different. Fundamentally, however, all our struggles are the same: figuring out how to honor God in a world that seems to punish us just for living.

The "spirit of the gospel," however, reminds us that there is supernatural comfort to be found from the gospel's Holy Spirit.

Supernatural Comfort Through the Gospel

In chapter 7 I shared with you my conversation with a young man struggling with feeling loved. At that same conference, I spoke with another young man with a different but related struggle. This fellow had suffered from a mental disability all his life. In a not-so-distant age, we would have classified him as "mentally retarded." But what he lacked in intellectual capability he did not in theological insight. He said to me that sometimes he asks God why he had to be born with his disability. His brother, he told me, is a smart engineer but an atheist. He said, "Sometimes I ask God, 'Why?'"

So I asked him, "What answer does God give you?"

He paused for a couple of seconds and finally answered, "Just that he loves me."

That was one of the most profound things I've ever heard.

See, we may not always (or ever) understand the ways of God's providence, why he makes us certain ways or leads us through certain things. But one thing we can know, looking at the cross—we are very *loved*.

This is perhaps the chief way the Holy Spirit comforts us in our afflictions. He reminds us of what Christ has done for us. And this is not because the Spirit is at a loss as to how to encourage us. He's not like our well-meaning friends who like to spout cheap inspirational clichés and lame pick-me-ups, mainly out of their own discomfort at our pain. He knows the biggest help we could ever get is from the power of the gospel. And the Spirit's reminding us of the gospel is entirely according to plan, just as Jesus said, "But the Helper, the Holy Spirit, whom the Father will send in my name, he will teach you all things and bring to your remembrance all that I have said to you" (John 14:26).

The Holy Spirit comes to us in our moments of suffering—even entering our suffering with us—and reminds us of the sufferings of Christ *for us*, that we are not alone now or ever because of the great and eternal love of God given to us through Jesus. Another way to put this is that the Holy Spirit comforts us by reminding us of God's love.

It is very tempting, especially in times of darkness, to feel abandoned or unloved. Even if others are showing us love, we may doubt the love of God because of the pains we face that only he can alleviate. For some reason he won't. We begin to reason, like Job's friends, that we have done something to deserve our disability, our depression, our debilitating pains. But the same Spirit who groans with us in Romans 8:26 reminds us of Romans 8:1: "There is therefore now no condemnation for those who are in Christ Jesus."

Our great Helper gently and firmly teaches us about Christ, bringing to our remembrance all Christ did for us, including dying. If you are ever tempted to doubt God's love for you, look at the cross!

The love of God is the most precious thing any person could ever know. It will sustain you like nothing else can and when nothing else will. It will encourage you through the darkest moments of your life. The love of God was put on you, child of God, before the world was even created, and it will carry you through your dying day and into the blissful joy of eternal reunion with the very source of love himself.

"God is love," wrote the apostle John (1 John 4:8). In the Trinity, the Father, the Son, and the Holy Spirit share an abounding love for each other that has overflowed and spilled into the bounds of creation, bringing even sinners like us to taste the goodness of God's divine nature.

The love of God, the psalmist said, is better than your next breath (Ps. 63:3), and so when all else gives way, whether you die young or old, when your eyes close each time in anguished prayer or for the final time, and your lungs give their final whisper, and your heart gives its last beat, the love of God will still be there, never stopping, never ending, lifting you up to glory. And on the day of resurrection, when you enjoy the fullness of creation in a restored earth, it will be love that empowers you and all the redeemed creation, and it will be the love of God that drives our worship of Jesus forever.

When you're tempted to think God has reached his limit with you, the Spirit reminds you, "The steadfast love of the Lord never ceases; his mercies never come to an end" (Lam. 3:22).

When you feel as though God has abandoned you, the Spirit reminds you, "The Lord is near to the brokenhearted and saves the crushed in spirit" (Ps. 34:18).

When you expect to be rejected by Christ, the Spirit reminds you that Jesus has gone to prepare a place for you, that where he is, you will be also (John 14:3).

When you are racked by insecurity, the Spirit reminds you that you are safely in the hands of Jesus and nothing can snatch you away (John 10:29).

When you are overcome by fear, the Spirit reminds you

that "perfect love casts out fear" (1 John 4:18) and that his own indwelling presence in your life is not conducive to fear, but to power, love, and self-control (2 Tim. 1:7). Indeed, "you did not receive the spirit of slavery to fall back into fear, but you have received the Spirit of adoption as sons" (Rom. 8:15).

When you are just flat-out overwhelmed by life, and you're tired and desperate and feel hopelessly lost, the Spirit reminds you that "neither death nor life, nor angels nor rulers, nor things present nor things to come, nor powers, nor height nor depth, nor anything else in all creation, will be able to separate us from the love of God in Christ Jesus our Lord" (Rom. 8:38–39).

We could go on and on because the gospel goes on and on. And the Holy Spirit sent by Christ to comfort us *will* go on and on to apply it to our hearts in the pain of our darkest days. And when our darkest days are no more, we will go on and on, celebrating the gospel with him for all eternity.

In his touching book *Wednesdays Were Pretty Normal*, my friend Michael Kelley recounted the journey his family took with his son Joshua, who bravely battled leukemia. Part memoir of suffering, part reflection on the life of faith, *Wednesdays* is an unflinching and yet inspirational examination of the gospel's comfort during what is most parents' worst nightmare—the suffering of a child and the prospect of losing him. Near the end, in a chapter simply titled "Peace," Kelley wrote:

> Before everything happened with Joshua, long before the days of chemotherapy and heartache and loss, I used to wonder if I would have the strength to undergo severe testing of my faith. And truth be told, I wasn't sure.
>
> And you know what? I'm still not.

But I have come to believe that because God has valued us so much and because He is interested in making us whole and complete people blessed with every spiritual blessing in Christ, we can count on the grace we need from Him when we need it. . . .

By faith I believe that whatever happens in the future, the Lord will be faithful to dole out what I need when I need it. Enough grace to put one foot in front of the other. That brings a sense of wholeness not only because we lack nothing now but because we believe, by His grace, that we will lack nothing we need in the future. That kind of grace can keep you walking.[4]

I feel compelled to tell you that today Joshua is alive and well and, as of this writing, cancer free. Lord willing, we pray, he will be so permanently. But at the time Kelley "came to believe" there was grace enough, he didn't know that. The future was uncertain. It still is. And yet the gospel is sure. It provides a comfort beyond anything, a comfort that extends from eternity past to eternity future, and thus it extends to you *right now*.

Supernatural Comfort Through the Church

Here is another good reminder that we are not meant to do the Christian life alone. This is important to consider, because it is very often in our most painful moments that we seek to be alone most. Whether we feel hurt by those who try to sympathize or we simply don't think others could help even if they wanted to, pain has a very isolating effect on us. Pain is lonely.

The Holy Spirit through the gospel is forming the new

humanity we call the church, and this is his official and only ambassadorship for the kingdom of heaven. We are not to take lightly, then, when Isaiah 40 prophesies the kingdom that will come in and through Jesus, beginning with the words, "Comfort, comfort my people" (v. 1).

Yes, church should be *un*comfortable for all the reasons we might biblically expect: because sin is challenged and confessed there, because struggles and fears are honestly shared there, because you can't get a bunch of sinners together and always expect things to go smoothly. But the prevailing message the church is meant both to share and embody is the comfort of grace.

Remember that even the persecuted church in Acts 9 was being built up and experiencing the comfort of the Spirit (v. 31). I imagine that a huge part of this comfort being felt was the Spirit working through the individual members of the body to comfort one another. Paul had this kind of interpersonal comfort in mind when he wrote 2 Corinthians 1:3–7:

> Blessed be the God and Father of our Lord Jesus Christ, the Father of mercies and God of all comfort, who comforts us in all our affliction, so that we may be able to comfort those who are in any affliction, with the comfort with which we ourselves are comforted by God. For as we share abundantly in Christ's sufferings, so through Christ we share abundantly in comfort too. If we are afflicted, it is for your comfort and salvation; and if we are comforted, it is for your comfort, which you experience when you patiently endure the same sufferings that we suffer. Our hope for you is unshaken, for we know that as you share in our sufferings, you will also share in our comfort.

That's a longish passage and maybe a little complex. To break it down, what Paul is saying is that because God comforts us by his Spirit, we are able to comfort others by his Spirit, and since this is the case, the church is a place where the Spirit comforts people *through* people.

Part of this comfort comes, as Paul indicates, in sharing our afflictions. Knowing that we are not alone, that our struggle isn't new or limited just to us, can be extremely encouraging. Of course people sometimes share information in insensitive ways. But when someone who has felt a similar pain is sensitively and compassionately able to become present in your pain, you feel the comfort of the Holy Spirit who is binding every believer together in love.

I have on occasion over the last several years made visits to a biblical counselor. I largely make these appointments for help in processing the general problem I like to call "being me." Because I have done a variety of kinds of mentoring, discipling, and pastoral counseling myself over the last twenty-plus years, I rarely hear anything in these sessions that is new or revolutionary. Most of the words of encouragement or advice I receive are things I am already aware of and inclined toward. But I still find these visits helpful because there is something powerful about grace announced that isn't exactly there in grace rehearsed.

As Dietrich Bonhoeffer said in his classic book on Christian fellowship, *Life Together*, "The Christ in his own heart is weaker than the Christ in the word of his brother,"[5] which is just an inverted way of saying that the gospel from his brother is stronger than the gospel in himself. This is only because the gospel is meant to be heard to be believed. And this too is a work of the Spirit.

Supernatural Comfort Through Christlikeness

Now here is something utterly unique: we might take some comfort not necessarily in the earthly relief of our pain but in the knowing that our pain is being stewarded heavenward, that we are in fact by our suffering becoming more like our Savior.

This is the kind of supernatural perspective cruelly avoided by the "health and wealth" preachers, who imagine that the Holy Spirit provides a kind of force field from pain. Some of these preachers even go so far as to say that faithful Christians can avoid getting diseases or getting sick. These extreme sorts claim to be laying hold of the promises of God, but they seem utterly ignorant of how all God's promises are connected to the cross of Christ. They want to skip over Good Friday and then turn resurrection Sunday into Easter baskets full of material goodies.

The best this backward theology can manage to do, however, is heap more pain on our pain, all the while cruelly promising peace. Author and *New York Times* columnist Ross Douthat summarized:

> At its best, the prosperity gospel can be well-meaning, open-handed, and personally empowering; and it thrives as few other forms of Christian faith do in the soil of modernity. But like many forms of liberal Christianity, the marriage of God and Mammon half-expects somehow to undo the Fall, through the beneficence of Providence and the magic of the free market. In its emphasis on the virtues of prosperity, it risks losing something essential to Christianity—skipping to Easter, you might say, without lingering at the foot of the cross.[6]

SUPERNATURAL POWER FOR EVERYDAY PEOPLE

Yes, the cross is a stake in the heart of the prosperity gospel. Even as it aims to highlight the supernatural wonders of the early church, the prosperity gospel simply cherry-picks from the book of Acts, digging up its Pentecostal climax from the poverty and persecution context. The cross is foolishness to the worldly wisdom of the prosperity gospel because it bids us find our joy, our satisfaction, our riches, and our victory in Christ alone, not in stuff. Because the cross gives us all things, we don't have to fear losing everything else, whether it be stuff or self.

Here is a great comfort for those who *feel* the death of the cross in all kinds of circumstances: you are becoming like Jesus. By beholding the glory of Christ, especially in our shared suffering with him, the Spirit is supernaturally transforming us into the image of our Savior (2 Cor. 3:18). He is making us like Jesus!

Isn't that what we want? To be made like Christ? This is in fact why the Son of God was made like us. He became the embodiment of our sin that we might experience, ultimately in our own bodies, the perfection of his righteousness (2 Cor. 5:21). There is no greater purpose we could hope to pursue. To be like Jesus is the only thing worth living for—or worth dying for.

Paul had this hope in mind when he wrote in Philippians 3 that he didn't care whether he lived or died, so long as he had Jesus. He said he was willing to lose admiration, status, financial and bodily security, supporters, and even his life in order that "I may know [Christ] and the power of his resurrection, and may share his sufferings, becoming like him in his death, that by any means possible I may attain the resurrection from the dead" (vv. 10–11).

Paul knew that to get to the power of the resurrection, he had to go through the pain of the cross. And he knew that because

Christ had taken the pain of the cross for him, he could gain the power of Christ's resurrection.

What a comfort this is! It may not alleviate our pain in the moment, but it certainly colors it with hope. As 2 Corinthians 1:5 reminds us, if we'll share in Christ's sufferings, we'll share in his comfort too. We'll share in the comfort of Christ in heaven, because those who suffer in his name will also enjoy the eternal life his name now proclaims. This light and momentary suffering will be nothing compared to the eternal weight of glory that awaits us at the end of our journey to Christlikeness.

Take comfort in this, Christian: every ounce of suffering will be compensated for with millions of years of rest, and still more besides. This suffering will be merely a blip on the radar of an eternity of peace, a grain of sand compared to the global beaches of God's comfort in the world to come.

Your suffering is storing up for you "the riches of the glory of this mystery"—namely, that Christ's image is being formed in you, and this is your "hope of glory" in the age to come (Col. 1:27). The comforting promise of the God of hope is to "fill you with all joy and peace in believing," so that by the supernatural power of the Holy Spirit you may abound in this hope (Rom. 15:13).

In your suffering, may you find comfort in knowing the Spirit is making you more like Christ.

Supernatural Comfort Through Spiritual Power

But wait, there's more. Returning to Acts 9, we notice in verse 22 that "Saul increased all the more in strength." We could spiritualize this, but let's capital *S* Spiritualize this—Saul was experiencing *felt* supernatural power from the Holy Spirit of God.

Make no mistake, you don't need to feel God's love to know it and own it. You may feel far from God though he is very close to you. You may feel the Spirit is distant though he has taken up residence in your heart. These are normal experiences of normal human life in our abnormal world. But at other times Christians indeed have a true and felt sense of the Spirit's working.

This sense may be experienced as an otherwise unexplainable inner peace or overflowing happiness. It may become manifest in a supernatural ability to withstand verbal or even spiritual or physical attacks. It may come at times when you are needing to share the gospel with someone or teach some believers or perform an act of service in the face of exhaustion. It may strike you in a word of encouragement to share with someone else in pain. Or it may be an overwhelming and awe-inspiring sense of the presence of the Holy God. When I had that moment of gospel wakefulness in that guest bedroom, I felt entirely different. I didn't become superhuman, of course, but I had a supernatural strength to resist sin in a new way, to endure my difficult circumstances with a new hope, to serve sacrificially with a new vigor. The feeling was real, and so were the effects of it. The Bible is full of these kinds of experiences. They may not be normative, but neither are they impossible. Why would we doubt their occurrence today?

None of these kinds of supernatural comfort should surprise us, really, given that the Holy Spirit himself is serving as our Advocate. He is constantly ministering to us and, now we know, even praying for us. How else he is administering the power of the gospel to our hearts and minds, we may not entirely know. This is always the case with the mysterious workings of the infinite God. Ray Ortlund wrote, "But *how* does the Holy Spirit help us? Now we enter into deep mystery. The Spirit helps us by interceding for us, Paul explains. When we are too defeated and confused to pray, when the familiar phrases just do not seem adequate any more, when all we can do is groan, the Spirit makes his own appeal on our behalf."[7]

But the Holy Spirit is no crutch. He is not helping you hobble along. In fact, what the Spirit is building in you and planning through you, even in your ordinary life, is so extraordinary you need his supernatural help to believe it!

CHAPTER 9

FINDING THE ENERGY TO GO THE DISTANCE

Experiencing the Spirit's Gifts

Now we are getting to the nitty-gritty. This chapter alone may be why you picked up this book. Have you been waiting for charismatic visions, words of knowledge, predictive prophecies, and tongues of fire?

Well, it is precisely the equation of supernatural power to these kinds of dramatic phenomena that prompted me to write this book in the first place, and why I chose to spend the first seven chapters speaking to the kinds of Spiritual power accessible to all believers at all times. But because no book on the Holy Spirit's power could be complete without a discussion of what are often called "charismatic gifts," I am here rewarding your patience with a (short) overview of that subject, and especially how it fits into the broader plan the Spirit has for the gospel in the world.

But first I want to test your patience just one more time. Don't worry, though: patience is one of the things the Holy Spirit supernaturally gives you!

What we have to get through our self-interested hearts is that nothing the Spirit gives us or does for us is meant to culminate in our own glory. Even when he is comforting us, strengthening us, guiding us, and enlightening us, he is doing so that we might better magnify Christ. It is for this reason that the Spirit is committed to us for the long haul.

What we are talking about here is called *sanctification*, the process by which we are being made holy by God's Spirit. God would not receive glory for saving a bunch of sinners who then became lost halfway through their journeys. So Jesus is committed not just to authoring our salvation but to perfecting it (Heb. 12:2), and the Spirit is committed to seeing that our justification is accompanied by our sanctification and ultimately our glorification (1 Cor. 6:11; Rom. 8:30).

Now, there is a sense in which we are sanctified all at once. This past tense sanctification happens at conversion when we repent of our sin and place our faith in Jesus Christ for forgiveness and eternal life. When we express saving faith in Christ, we are justified—declared righteous—and, because of the imputed righteousness of Christ inherent in our justification, also definitively sanctified—declared holy.

But those who have come to Christ know they still sin. (And anyone who denies that fact is guilty of an additional sin of lying.) So it is a marvelous gift of grace that the Holy Spirit doesn't simply apply the definitive past/future tense sanctification of the gospel to us, but also begins to apply the progressive present/future tense sanctification of the gospel to us. We see an echo of this in 1 Corinthians 15:1–2, where Paul says that the gospel we received (past conversion) is also the gospel in which we stand (present justification) and by which we are *being* saved (present/future sanctification).

The bottom line is this: God isn't simply content to *declare* us holy, as wonderful as that is—he is determined to *make* us holy!

Some strains of Christianity teach, because of the biblical teaching on progressive sanctification, a kind of perfectionism that posits the possibility of a Christian reaching sinlessness prior to death or Christ's return. But while the biblical teaching on progressive sanctification does show us that the Spirit is making Christians more like Christ—which should result in a lifetime of discipleship in noticeable victories over sinful thoughts and behavior patterns—we also know that we will not be free from all the sin that so easily entangles us until we are transposed to glory at our passing or Christ returns to finally vanquish sin and the devil forever.

In the meantime, what the Holy Spirit is doing is preparing us for a life meant to redound to the glory of Christ, the only truly sinless one. And he does this in two major ways in our lives: growing us up through Spiritual fruit and building us up through Spiritual gifts.

Supernatural Growth in Grace: The Fruit of the Spirit

"But I say, walk by the Spirit, and you will not gratify the desires of the flesh."

This was Paul writing in Galatians 5:16. He had just laid out an earth-shattering case against the legalism so insidious in our flesh and frequently in the church. Having just proclaimed the liberation of grace, he now urged his readers to keep in step with the Spirit, what he described earlier as walking "in step with the truth of the gospel" (2:14).

Whatever you are following will shape you. This is why Paul then commended being "led by the Spirit" (Gal. 5:18). If we follow the flesh, the natural result is something you might find in this list: sexual immorality, impurity, sensuality, idolatry, sorcery, enmity, strife, jealousy, fits of anger, rivalries, dissensions, divisions, envy, drunkenness, and orgies (5:19–21).

But then Paul offered a list of another kind. What happens "naturally" if you are led by the Spirit? Love, joy, peace, patience, kindness, goodness, faithfulness, gentleness, and self-control (5:22–23).

Notice that the first list—the works of the flesh—represents a wide variety of sins. Drunkenness to jealousy. Sexual immorality to fits of anger. Some of these sins are easy to hide; some are not. And Paul left out nothing. Categorically speaking, Paul's list of sins runs the gamut. There's no way for you to feel like you and your special sin have found the loophole. (And even if you think you have, Paul adds a helpful "and things like these" at the end, anyway.)

The other thing I notice about the two contrasting lists is this: the first consists largely of actions, while the second consists largely of qualities, conditions. The first list corresponds to bad things to do, while the second list corresponds to good things to be.

We are seeing again how the gospel goes deeper than the law. The solution to the bad things *done* is to *become* good things.

Modifying our behavior is fairly easy. I know religious people who don't have affairs, don't get drunk, and don't mess around with pornography, but are loveless, joyless, impatient, unkind, and ungentle.

The effect we want is to think, talk, and act differently—to be workers of holiness instead of iniquity—but the way to do that is to *be* different people. So Paul said in verse 16, "Walk by the Spirit, and you will not gratify the desires of the flesh." Something happens when the Spirit takes the lead. We certainly change our behavior, but we do so because of an inward power to transform, not because of some outward pressure to conform.

In Paul's way of thinking here, it is not that we aren't doing something. We are. We're walking (5:16), we're following a lead (5:18), and we're keeping in step with the Spirit (5:25). We're not passive. But the real work of transformation is coming by the Spirit through the gospel. And just as that gospel is like a mustard seed that becomes a tree big enough for all the birds of the air to come make their nests, the gospel is like a seed in our hearts that, cultivated by the Spirit, grows into an amazing harvest of precious fruit.

By faith in the Son's work, you stand before God now totally justified, totally qualified, and totally energized to walk by the Spirit of truth given to you through the gospel and to take dominion for it in all areas of your life.

In a way, by producing this fruit in us, the Holy Spirit is replicating the work of the Son. The growth in grace that is characterized by the fruit of the Spirit is an important aspect of our sanctification, becoming more like Christ. For who exemplifies these attributes better than Christ himself? Who has ever been more loving, more joyful, more peaceful, more patient, more kind, more upright, more faithful, more gentle, and more self-controlled than Jesus?

The Spirit's production of this fruit in our lives is enabling us to better obey our Lord and follow his example. Dallas Willard agrees, writing, "By not walking in terms of the flesh but in terms of the Spirit, we are increasingly able to do the things that Jesus did and taught."[1]

The only way, in fact, to become like Jesus in a genuine way is to be supernaturally transformed. We learn from Paul's writing on the fruit of the Spirit that God is determined to activate this fruit in our lives, which, in turn will help us to honor God with our obedience and love our neighbor with our service.

But there is still more of the supernatural to lay hold of.

Supernatural Acts of Grace: The Gifts of the Spirit

What does the exercise of the Spiritual gifts look like for so-called ordinary Christians today? Does it look any different than it did for Christians of yesterday? Are all the gifts available to believers? Or just some of them? If just some, how do we know which ones? If we only admit the less "strange" gifts, what is our basis for picking and choosing this way? Are most of our evangelical aversions to exotic manifestations of the Spirit based on theological arguments or cultural assumptions or both?

Before I put all my cards out on the table, I'll do a little background work. What follows should not be taken as an exhaustive treatment of this subject. It will be an overview, and admittedly it will be representative of my own viewpoint. For those interested in fuller treatments of this particular aspect of the Spirit's work, please consult the Recommended Reading section at the end of the book.

What is a spiritual gift? Would it surprise you to know that the word from which we get the category "spiritual gift" is the Greek *charism* or *charismata*? Would it surprise you to know that this phrase is used for all the spiritual gifts, not just the more dramatic sign gifts? The gifts of teaching, mercy, encouragement, and discernment, strictly speaking, are charismatic gifts. They all are *charismata*.

The other Greek word often found behind these gifts is *pneumatikos*, which literally means "work of the spirit." Theologian Wayne Grudem defined all these spiritual gifts as "any ability that is empowered by the Holy Spirit and used in any ministry of the church."[2] The list of acts falling under the broad category of spiritual gifts can be culled from passages in 1 Corinthians 12, Romans 12, and 1 Peter 4, and includes the following:

prophecy
teaching
faith
miracles
healings
helps
administration
tongues and interpretation of tongues
words of wisdom
words of knowledge
discernment
evangelism
service

encouragement and exhortation
generosity
leadership
mercy
hospitality

From the contexts surrounding these various named gifts, we get the sense that they may vary in strength and variety from person to person, church to church. I am of the mind that all gifts are exercisable at the Spirit's discretion by all Christians under a given set of circumstances, but it seems obvious to me that some Christians are more gifted than others in certain areas. In other words, every Christian should have the opportunity to practice evangelism and hospitality and service, but some Christians are particularly adept at these gifts. Every Christian may be empowered by the Spirit in some way to teach in certain circumstances (their children, someone they're discipling, etc.), but others have a more pronounced gift that enables them to fulfill certain roles in the church that call for regular teaching or that helps qualify them for the office of pastor.

Limiting our viewpoints on individual Christian giftedness is unbiblical and therefore unwise, and can lead to believers shirking their responsibility to exercise certain gifts that help to fulfill Christ's commands. For instance, I do not get to "opt out" of sharing the gospel with others by claiming I lack the gift of evangelism. You don't get to opt out of treating people with mercy because you didn't identify that gift in your last spiritual gift survey.

All of the gifts are available to all Christians at the Spirit's discretion in certain circumstances, and yet most Christians will be more adept or given (super)naturally to a certain gift or set of gifts. For example, after thirty-plus years of walking with Christ and almost that long serving his church, I know I am more strongly gifted in teaching, prophecy (of the nonprescient kind), and discernment. My wife, on the other hand, is more strongly gifted in hospitality, helps, and administration.

The variety and strength of gifts reflect the diversity within the body of Christ along the lines of personality, interest, and temperament. God has made each of us unique, and he strengthens us for service to the church in different ways.

In regard to what are sometimes known as sign gifts (often called the "charismatic gifts," although it bears repeating that all the gifts are *charismata*)—miracles, healing, words of knowledge, prophecy (of the prescient kind), various tongues—most believers fall into two broad categories of thinking:

Cessationists are those who believe that the sign gifts have ceased (thus, cessation), either at the end of the first apostolic age or upon the official identifying and closing of the New Testament canon. Most cessationists will not argue against the idea that the Spirit is free to do as he wishes and that instances of charismatic phenomena may be granted in certain situations, most often, for instance, on the mission field. But generally speaking, cessationists would argue not only that the sign gifts are not normative for the church but that they are for all intents and purposes not operational. The primary concern here, and it is a valuable one, is for the sufficiency of Scripture.

On the other side of the ideological aisle are the *continuationists*, who believe that all the gifts are still functioning today in the ongoing church age. Those who personally practice these gifts I categorize colloquially as *charismatics*. All charismatics are by definition continuationists, but not all continuationists are charismatics. One can believe that all the gifts are operational in the church today but not personally practice them or even fellowship in a church that practices them.

I fall into the noncharismatic continuationist camp. My reasons break down into three major arguments: experiential, historical, and biblical. Below I will offer some thoughts on each major argument, moving in that order, which I consider to be from weakest (experiential) to strongest (biblical).

The Experiential Argument for the Continuation of the Charismatic Gifts

I think of friends and colleagues throughout my life and ministry who were not only continuationists but practicing charismatics. I also think of several "famous" charismatics who are well-regarded teachers and preachers within the realm of orthodox evangelicalism. Thinking logically as a cessationist, I am forced to consider only a few options about their claims to operate regularly in the gifts—they are lying, faking, or influenced by demons (or perhaps merely psychological illness).

What seems the most likely scenario?

I think of some dear folks I have pastored. One woman in particular was the sweetest woman I have ever met, and not sweet in the sentimental, cutesy way, but sweet in the Spirit, willing to help anyone at any time with anything, sweet in prayer and service to the church. You would never know she possessed the gift of tongues, because she didn't really tell anybody that. She didn't practice this gift in public worship, nor had she ever asked if she could. Most people didn't even know, and I suppose I only knew because as her pastor I was privy to more information than most.

Most of my friends who practice the gifts are the same way:

humble, unassuming, gentle practitioners of gifts they would never use as leverage in the church for their own worship preferences or self-fulfillment. These men and women of God exhibit most visibly the fruit of the Spirit, not these dramatic gifts.

I find simply dismissing their practice very difficult. And I have yet to hear a compelling cessationist argument on this matter. Some noted cessationists in public ministry are utterly convinced that the charismatic gifts are a satanic counterfeit in the church today, and yet they continue fellowship with and admiration for noted charismatics. I find this puzzling. Sometimes a cessationist will express "caution" to his charismatic friends about their views, but I've never heard any cessationist give an outright explanation of what he thinks his friends are practicing. Are they deceived? Are they hoaxers? If so, why admire them?

Many of us are also privy to reports from the mission field, where the sign gifts seem more readily accessed and received. I am not prepared to throw out all of these testimonies. Certainly some are suspect. Certainly the Devil can work wonders in order to counterfeit the work of God and attempt to derail it. But many reports come firsthand from reliable, mature sources. It's possible the gifts are more normative in circumstances where the gospel of the kingdom is first breaking into a previously unreached people group. This would resemble more the missional context of the apostolic ministry in Acts, to be sure. But it would also seem to weaken the cessationist argument that the gifts aren't normative *anywhere*.

The Historical Argument for the Continuation of the Charismatic Gifts

There is no denying that the evidence for the avid practice of the charismatic gifts throughout church history is not substantial.

On the other hand, however, the evidence does exist. While there may be reasons we do not see the gifts emphasized in certain ages of church history,[3] I don't believe we have solid reasons to discount their practice entirely. We see examples from early church fathers, such as Justin Martyr, Irenaeus, and Eusebius, evidencing the presence of sign gifts in their contemporary ministries. One of the early church's heresy hunters, Epiphanius, was one of the biggest critics of the Montanists, a late second-century religious sect characterized by its charismatic enthusiasm. But according to Sam Storms, Epiphanius "did not attack them because they practiced the gifts of the Spirit,"[4] for Epiphanius himself declared that "God's holy church also receives the gifts of grace—but the real gifts, which have already been tried in God's holy church through the Holy Spirit."[5]

Saint Augustine, who was perhaps the greatest early church father and himself a cessationist at the start of his ministry, eventually noted at least seventy instances of miraculous healings within a two-year ministry time frame in his epic book *The City of God*.[6]

We have other isolated examples leading out of the apostolic age, through the patristic era and medieval eras, even through the days of the Reformation to more recent church history. Manifestations of sign gifts and other charismatic expressions were present at some of the gatherings within the first Great Awakening in 1730s and 1740s America, which were mostly associated with Jonathan Edwards, himself not known as an overly charismatic personality! More recently, Charles Spurgeon noted in his autobiography several instances of receiving words of knowledge.

All of these instances and more, put together, do not make

for us an airtight case. Yet neither do they lend credence to the idea that church history knows nothing of the charismatic gifts after the apostolic age or the closing of the canon. D. A. Carson concurred: "What can be safely concluded from the historical evidence? First, there is enough evidence that some form of 'charismatic' gifts continued sporadically across the centuries of church history that it is futile to insist on doctrinaire grounds that every report is spurious or the fruit of demonic activity or psychological aberration."[7]

No, I don't believe we can make a compelling historical argument that the charismatic gifts have ceased altogether. But, like charismatic gifts, experiential and historical arguments mean nothing if they do not conform to the rightly interpreted teaching of the Scriptures. The Bible really is sufficient.

So what does it say?

The Biblical Argument for the Continuation of the Charismatic Gifts

This argument will not convince everyone, if only because of its brevity and exegetical broad strokes. But let's start with perhaps the central biblical text at hand, the passage that allegedly speaks to the cessation of the charismatic gifts.

Love never ends. As for prophecies, they will pass away; as for tongues, they will cease; as for knowledge, it will pass away. For we know in part and we prophesy in part, but when the perfect comes, the partial will pass away. When I was a child, I spoke like a child, I thought like a child, I reasoned like a child. When I became a man, I gave up childish ways. For now we see in a mirror dimly, but then face to face. Now I know in part; then I shall know fully, even as I have been fully known. (1 Cor. 13:8–13)

Cessationists usually argue that "the perfect" Paul was writing about here in verse 10 refers to the closing of the New Testament canon. And we can certainly draw some parallels between the metaphors Paul was using—seeing clearly, knowing fully—and the finality and sufficiency of the written Word of God. And yet the metaphors seem to draw our vision to an even still future time. I find the phrase "but then face to face" more directly applicable to understanding what is meant by "when the perfect comes." And I think a better explanation for what Paul is envisioning here is the day when he (and we) finally meet Jesus face-to-face, whether at his return or our passing into glory.

The operational contrast in this passage, then, does not appear to be between having part of the Scriptures now versus all of them later but between knowing Jesus through our earthly, fallen experience now versus finally being reunited with him when his kingdom is consummated.

This argument makes the most sense, too, of all the instructions given concerning the gifts, especially in the ensuing chapter. If those gifts are soon to be unnecessary, why would Paul give such extensive commands concerning their appropriate use to be included in the very canon that allegedly would, once closed, preclude their use?

Much more can be said, but this is the crux of the textual matter for me. Given all that Paul says about the gifts here and elsewhere, I find it exegetically untenable to believe there is no direct import for the church centered on God's Word today. It would make large portions of the New Testament letters to the churches less applicable to the modern churches than most of the ancient history in the Old Testament. And there is no one clear "gotcha" cessationist passage anyway. The primary exegetical argument largely hinges on one phrase that in context does not say what it is claimed to say.

But none of that gets to the heart of the real matter of this book. You and I are not chasing theoretical arguments about the Spirit. We are ordinary people interested in supernatural power! So, given my thesis that the charismatic gifts have not ceased, what do we do with them?

The answer may vary from person to person and church to church.[8] But the latter context is most important. The point of the Spiritual gifts is the same as the Spiritual fruit—to serve others and build up Christ's church. Paul wrote this in the preceding chapter: "Now concerning spiritual gifts, brothers, I do not want you to be uninformed. You know that when you were pagans you were led astray to mute idols, however you were led. Therefore I want you to understand that no one speaking in the Spirit of God ever says 'Jesus is accursed!' and no one can say 'Jesus is Lord' except in the Holy Spirit" (1 Cor. 12:1–3).

This reminds us that, first and most importantly, all gifts granted by the Spirit are given so that Christ Jesus will receive glory. We are not given any gift—whether teaching or tongues, works of service or words of knowledge—to glorify ourselves. The Spiritual gifts aren't keys to becoming super-Christians. They are distributed mainly that we might contribute to the magnification of Jesus.

Paul continued, "Now there are varieties of gifts, but the

same Spirit; and there are varieties of service, but the same Lord; and there are varieties of activities, but it is the same God who empowers them all in everyone. To each is given the manifestation of the Spirit for the common good" (12:4–7).

So what are the gifts for? According to Paul, these are the purposes of all the gifts:

- to make manifest the glorious beauty of Jesus
- to serve the common good of the church
- to contribute to the work of ministry
- to provide a foretaste of the age to come

Mature, intelligent, Bible-believing Christians will continue to differ on the matter of the charismatic gifts, likely until the end of the age (when we finally see Jesus "face to face"!), but mature, intelligent, Bible-believing Christians should agree that the Scriptures are sufficient, that any alleged word or knowledge or revelation stands or falls under the authoritative and infallible Word of God. Nothing shall be added to it or subtracted from it. And it is from this sufficient Word that we also receive the following exhortations:

> Do not quench the Spirit. Do not despise prophecies, but test everything; hold fast what is good. (1 Thess. 5:19–21)
>
> Pursue love, and earnestly desire the spiritual gifts. (1 Cor. 14:1)

At the very least, what these instructions mean is that while exercising discernment and caution about the spectacular claims of human beings is always wise, we need never be afraid of the Holy Spirit. God can be trusted to work his will in ways both ordinary and extraordinary, and he does not leave it to us to decide which is which. Let's not, in other words, be timid where the Spirit has made us courageous. He is gifting us for the powerful work of making Jesus look big in the church and in the world.

CHAPTER 10

THE POWERFUL PROMISES OF GOD

Experiencing the Spirit's Baptism

There is nothing ordinary about the Christian.

Even before conversion, there is really nothing ordinary about human beings, for we are created in the image of God. Despite our sin, our fallen mortality, and our fleshly propensity for brokenness and chaos, we are fearfully and wonderfully made. God has made all people, saints and sinners, just a little lower than the angels, the crown of his good creation. So we start this journey born in sin but already exceptional. This alone is a wonder.

But then there is the gospel! For as exceptional as human beings can manage to be, not even the best of us can manage holiness. We all are objects of wrath destined for destruction, not because each of us is as bad as we could possibly be, but because none of us comes remotely close to the goodness of God. His holiness is perfect, and nothing sinful can stand in his presence. But that gospel. Oh my. That good news comes sailing out of the sky, the glorious forethought from eternity past made manifest in God's Son, born as a baby to be the Messiah, our King, our Redeemer.

And the Holy Spirit of God is always in the thick of it, wooing and winning, enlightening and empowering. The Holy Spirit applies this gospel to us once for all time and paradoxically continues to apply it still further to us, again and again, until our cup overflows with "grace upon grace" (John 1:16). I have tried to demonstrate from page 1 of this book onward how the Spirit is committed to revealing and administering Christ's finished work in our lives. Thus far we have seen how the Spirit

- convicts us of our sinful self-sovereignty and self-sufficiency,
- empowers us in ways that are surprising and eternal,
- guides us through a world of idolatrous noise in the Godward way of the kingdom,
- strengthens us through the spiritual disciplines of prayer and Scripture reading,
- fills us when we repent of finding satisfaction in anyone or anything other than him,
- counsels us through the difficulty of broken relationships and personal conflict,
- comforts us in our deepest pains and darkest moments, and
- gifts us for growth and vitality in the Christian life and church.

But the Spirit who is God goes much further in relation to sinners who believe in Jesus. The gospel could not be contained in nine *thousand* chapters! Certainly nine cannot do justice to the Spirit's work in salvation.

What more has God promised us in and through his Holy Spirit?

A Tour de Force of the Spirit's Gospel Promises

In the beginning, the Holy Spirit was hovering over the surface of the deep. He separated land from sea, order from chaos. The Spirit, along with the Father and the Son, orchestrated the establishment of creation. They spoke it into existence. It didn't exist, and then it did. *Super*natural.

The Spirit spoke to our forefathers, the patriarchs of old. In bushes and in wind, in fire and in clouds. The Spirit led the people of God into the wilderness, hovered over their tabernacle, came to rest on the mercy seat. The blood of lambs, the harvest of fields, hammered metals and engraved wood—the Spirit took what was natural and stewarded it for glory. *Super*natural.

The Spirit inspired the prophets, sending fiery altars and fiery words. The Spirit stirred up visions of mountains, of dancing bones, of wheels within wheels. The Spirit sent the messages of truth to power: repent, return, renew, restore. He did this through shepherds and fig growers and backwoods farmers. *Super*natural.

And then there was silence. For four hundred years, actual silence. All the people of God had was what he had already said. The promises felt unfulfilled. Until . . .

The Spirit stirred up a baby and then conceived his cousin in a virgin womb. One paved the way, and the other *was* the Way. "The Spirit of the Lord is upon me," our Lord read aloud in the temple (Luke 4:18), announcing that all the Spirit's work in foretelling and preparing the kingdom had finally come. And while our great God and Savior, Jesus Christ, returned to his Father, our great God and Helper, the Holy Spirit, remains. And his ministry of Christ's glorification continues to advance, as it has from the beginning.

The Spirit Is Present in the Gospel

Yes, it was the Spirit who administered the incarnation of the Son (Matt. 1:18–20). And the Spirit's anointing of Christ's entire ministry—which becomes our righteousness through faith—never waned thereafter. The Spirit descended like a dove at Jesus' baptism (Mark 1:10). The Spirit led Jesus into the wilderness to be tempted by the Devil (Matt. 4:1). By the Spirit, Jesus cast out spiritual darkness (Matt. 12:28). It was the Spirit whom Jesus found comfort thinking of before his anguished prayer in the Garden of Gethsemane (John 14–17). The Spirit received him at his death and later resurrected him (1 Peter 3:18). And Jesus sent the Spirit at his ascension to the right hand of the Father (Acts 1:1–9). The Spirit was officially released from heaven at Pentecost. It was not as if God's people had no access to the Spirit before this moment, but the difference is like that between a steadily trickling mountain stream and a mighty, rushing flood through a busted dam. Ever since, the Spirit's presence in the world has been to ensure the spread of the gospel of God's glory, that someday this glory will cover the earth as the waters cover the sea (Hab. 2:14).

The Spirit Enables Belief

We see in Acts 13:48 that those who come to believe were "appointed to" this belief beforehand. In 1 Corinthians 2:14 we learn that the person without the Spirit cannot discern the things of God. Only through the Spirit can a person discern the wisdom of the gospel and place faith in Christ. So we see that even conversion must be enabled by the Spirit.

The Spirit Opens Our Eyes to See Christ

The way the Spirit enables conversion is by regenerating our hearts, opening the "eyes" of our hearts to behold the glory of Christ as beautiful and saving. Paul discusses this wonderful supernatural truth in 2 Corinthians 3, specifically in verse 18, where we learn that it's by beholding the glory of Christ that we are transformed. In verse 3, he says all this is wrought by the Spirit of the living God.

The Spirit Indwells Us

Oh, what a remarkable truth this is that the Spirit indwells us! Strange and inconceivable, and yet remarkably true! We learn from the Scriptures—for instance, 1 Corinthians 6:19 and 2 Timothy 1:14—that the Spirit doesn't just awaken our souls to desire Jesus, he takes up residence in our souls to satisfy us with the goodness of Jesus we now desire. From his place inside the temple of our bodies, the Spirit seeds good fruit, shapes godly thoughts, and empowers holy living.

The Spirit Pours Love into Our Hearts

Romans 5:5 says, "God's love has been poured into our hearts through the Holy Spirit who has been given to us." I'm not sure

I've ever met a person who felt too loved. Have you? What about too full of the love of God? The notion is nonsensical. The love of God cannot corrupt us but only cleanse us and change us, and now we know that the Spirit of God is committed to filling us continually in our insidest insides with the love of God.

The Spirit Gives Us Assurance

Can we know that we are saved? Salvation is not simply about a feeling; it's about a legal testimony, a supernaturally pronounced truth about something Christ did in history. Yes, we can know that we are saved, because as Romans 8:16 tells us, God's Spirit bears witness with our own spirits that we are God's children.

The Spirit Empowers Our Prayers

Jude's phrase "praying in the Holy Spirit" (v. 20) suggests that the Holy Spirit is part of the predestining, prompting, and presenting of our prayers to the Father.

The Spirit Gives Us Unction

Every seasoned preacher knows what it means to receive the unction of the Spirit. Sometimes you are just minding your own homiletical business, going through your manuscript, and you inadvertently hit the jet stream. The Lord gives you some oomph. The words come easily, cleanly. The people respond attentively and joyfully. The gospel rings with clarity and power. What has happened? The Spirit has given you an extra dose of filling; he's given your gospel preaching unction. We see this phenomena suggested in the Scriptures every time we see the Spirit described as "rushing upon," "coming upon," or "anointing" someone, or whenever someone is described as carrying out a particular task "full of the Spirit."

The Spirit Revives the Church

Revival is the desire of my heart for our day. Don't we desperately need it? The evangelical church in the West is becoming less evangelical, perhaps less Christian. All of our pragmatic techniques and visionary strategies haven't seemed to stir up revival. We've been able to build some big churches, but the number of professing Christians is still in decline. Something doesn't add up. What could we possibly need right now more than a genuine move of the Holy Spirit in our land, beginning with God's people? Yes, we need a revival. And that's not something we can get by putting it on the church calendar or a roadside sign. Only the Holy Spirit can bring revival.

The Spirit Writes the Law on Our Hearts

The Spirit writes the letter of Christ not on stone tablets but on our hearts (2 Cor. 3:3). God says, according to Ezekiel 36:27, "I will put my Spirit within you, and cause you to walk in my statutes and be careful to obey my rules." The Spirit writing the Law on our hearts has the double effect of declaring us righteous in Christ and imparting the knowledge and power to live righteously in a way that honors Christ.

The Spirit Creates Good Works for Us to Do

Ephesians 2:10 says that even our good works aren't really our good ideas—they were created by God beforehand, predestined for us, that we might, in a way, step into them. I find this incredibly helpful to know because it means that if I'm a genuine

Christian, I will bear fruit! The Holy Spirit empowers me for this; he is doing good in the world through me.

The Spirit Causes Us to Abound in Hope

That the Holy Spirit causes us to abound in hope is not the last word by far, but it is still a fitting close to our tour de force of gospel promises: Romans 15:13 says that the power of the Holy Spirit makes us abound in hope. This is the antidote to the bad news on cable news networks. This is the answer to the bad news on that medical report. This is the answer to that deep longing, that gnawing pain, that nagging sense that something isn't quite right.

When you're feeling hopeless and those motivational posters aren't working, what do you need? You need power—supernatural power. You need supernatural power to cause you to hope again, to *abound* in hope.

The Baptism of the Holy Spirit

In Psalm 51 David was in spiritual anguish. He was buckling under the weight of his sin, both the guilt of it and the stain of it. And he said something very insightful, something that cuts to the heart of all we've journeyed through in this consideration of supernatural power for ordinary people. The worst thing David could think of happening to him was not that he would be caught or not that his reputation would be ruined. It was not even feeling guilty or being punished. The worst thing David could conceive of happening to him was that he would not have the Holy Spirit. "Cast me not away from your presence, and take not your Holy Spirit from me" (51:11).

We may suppose that, theologically, David knew this was not a possibility. In fact, we know from another of David's psalms (Psalm 139) that he was a firm believer in both the omnipresence of God's Spirit and the immanence of God's Spirit. But in his anguished state, desperate for grace and restoration, he was stripped down to the most fundamental human desire: to know and be known by God intimately, personally, for God to come near and fellowship with him. We all want, deep down, to be friends with God.

David's worst nightmare was to live one second apart from the powerful presence of the Holy Spirit. It ought to be ours as well.

If you are a Christian—if you've repented of your sin and placed your faith in Jesus Christ to receive his sinless life, sacrificial death, and glorious resurrection for your own—you are forgiven and free and you are fellowshiping with God. Right now. Right this very second you are enjoying God's presence, closer than the hair on your head and the skin on your bones.

And this is what the Holy Spirit is committed to doing in your life: making you more and more aware of your closeness with God through union with Christ and continually making you holier as the outworking of that union. Richard Lovelace wrote, "The apprehension of God's presence is the ultimate core of genuine Christian experience."[1]

Do you apprehend God's presence?

The promise of God's presence has been sounded loud and clear. Jesus said he would send you his Spirit. And to anyone who believes in him, he has granted this promise.

He has even promised that we would be baptized by the Holy Spirit. What on earth can that mean?

Well, it's not really something on earth but rather something in heaven. The baptism of the Holy Spirit is the believer's immersion into the life of the Spirit. It is a subsuming of our spirit by the Spirit of heaven, making us citizens of heaven as we live and breathe today! Because of the baptism of the Holy Spirit, you are not just sitting in that chair right now reading this book, but are also "seated . . . with him in the heavenly places" (Eph. 2:6). It is because of the baptism of the Holy Spirit that you are not just tucked into your bed right now reading this book, but also "tucked into" God with his Son Christ Jesus (Col. 3:3).

Does the baptism of the Holy Spirit happen at conversion, or is it something secondary? Yes.

You don't have to speak in tongues to be baptized in the Holy Spirit, and you don't have to have some religious spokesperson lay his hands on you to receive the baptism of the Holy Spirit, and you don't have to go into a trance or pray yourself into convulsions or "let go and let God" or any of that. You just have to repent of your sin and place your faith in Christ Jesus. You fire the board members at that conference table in your soul, knock down all the cubicle walls, and open yourself up to the fullness of Christ's love for every square inch of your life.

You take up your cross and follow Jesus.

Baptism in the Holy Spirit is the indwelling, outworking, all-impacting presence of God's Spirit in your life. Craig Keener wrote:

> The baptism in the Holy Spirit includes God's empowerment for the mission he has given us, his church. . . . God has made us new by his Spirit and now enables us to live holy lives and build up our fellow believers by the Spirit's fruit and gifts (Paul). God has

washed us, causing us to be born from him with a new character
(John). Through the empowerment of God's Spirit, we are called
to take Jesus' message both to those around us and to the ends
of the earth (Acts). Through the empowerment of God's Spirit,
Jesus prepares us to face the conflicts involved in our mission,
confronting and defeating the devil at the point of human need
(Mark). The Spirit transforms us when we come to Christ; from
that point forward we must continue to depend on his power to
carry out the mission Jesus gave us.[2]

Keener was making the case that, given all the ways the
baptism of the Holy Spirit is described in the New Testament,
it is shortsighted to relegate the experience to one particular
instance. More likely, the baptism of the Holy Spirit is given to
the believer at the new birth, when the Spirit remakes our heart,
one that desires and trusts in Jesus. But we know that the Spirit
does not stop his ministry to us there. He continues to convict us,
counsel us, comfort us, and consecrate us, that we might become
more and more surrendered to his leading and more and more
reflective of our Savior. This process can be seen as a deeper and
deeper immersion in the depths of grace.

We don't get any more "saved"—at least, not in the sense that
when we are first converted our salvation is in some kind of jeop-
ardy of not "sticking." There is no justification 2.0. Those whom
the Lord justifies he sanctifies and will glorify. So you are every
day as a believer experiencing more of the Spirit's baptizing. In
fact, every day you get out of bed and yawn, you're receiving
those gifts from the Spirit (Job 33:4).

Remember our friend Bill? He has a long life ahead of him,
a lot more time to grow in his newly revived faith. But he doesn't

know that, just as none of us knows when our time to get called up will come. So Bill has decided to make the most of the time that has been given to him. Every day he wakes up is a gift. And he's tired of wasting it living for himself, thinking only of himself or thinking of nothing at all.

Autopilot Bill has been fired. The time has come to walk by the Spirit.

And the Holy Spirit, who is God, can be trusted. He can be trusted, above all, to lovingly provide us with all we need for all our days—and then some.

"If you then, who are evil, know how to give good gifts to your children, how much more will the heavenly Father give the Holy Spirit to those who ask him!" (Luke 11:13).

RECOMMENDED READING

Jerry Bridges, *The Fruitful Life* (NavPress)

Jerry Bridges and Bob Bevington, *The Bookends of the Christian Life* (Crossway)

D. A. Carson, *Showing the Spirit* (Baker)

Francis Chan, *The Forgotten God* (David C. Cook)

Jonathan Edwards, *The Distinguishing Marks of a Work of the Spirit of God*

Sinclair Ferguson, *The Holy Spirit* (InterVarsity)

Billy Graham, *The Holy Spirit* (Thomas Nelson)

J. D. Greear, *Jesus Continued: Why the Spirit Inside You Is Better Than Jesus Beside You* (Zondervan)

Craig S. Keener, *Gift and Giver: The Holy Spirit for Today* (Baker)

Ronald A. N. Kydd, *Charismatic Gifts in the Early Church* (Hendrickson)

Richard Lovelace, *Dynamics of Spiritual Life* (InterVarsity)

Raymond C. Ortlund Jr., *Supernatural Living for Natural People* (Christian Focus)

John Owen, *Communion with the Triune God* (Crossway)

J. I. Packer, *Keep in Step with the Spirit* (Baker)

Michael Reeves, *Delighting in the Trinity* (InterVarsity)

Charles Spurgeon, *Holy Spirit Power* (Whitaker House)

Sam Storms, *Practicing the Power: Welcoming the Gifts of the Holy Spirit in Your Life* (Zondervan)

Joe Thorn, *Experiencing the Trinity* (Crossway)

Jared C. Wilson, *Gospel Wakefulness* (Crossway) and *The Imperfect Disciple* (Baker)

ACKNOWLEDGMENTS

Even authors who write by themselves do not write alone. I have been grateful through the duration of this project for the Holy Spirit's gracious encouragement given to me through a small army of precious souls camped on my side. The experienced input and savvy know-how from the good folks at Thomas Nelson has been a blessing.

After three projects together, I am increasingly thankful for the wise counsel and insight from my friend and agent, Don Gates. The stellar community at Midwestern Baptist Theological Seminary has provided the camaraderie and the charity through which to keep thinking and writing with confidence. Special thanks go to Dr. Christian George—our weekly meetings keep me going in ways more than creative. I am theologically and spiritually indebted to so many, including the gospel-rich community of brothers and sisters at Liberty Baptist Church in Kansas City.

Most of all, triple honor is due to Becky, Macy, and Grace, for all the leeway given while the man of the house trains yet another pet manuscript to obey his voice. I love you all.

ABOUT THE AUTHOR

Jared C. Wilson is the Director of Content Strategy at Midwestern Baptist Theological Seminary, Managing Editor of For The Church (ftc.co), and Director of the Pastoral Training Center at Liberty Baptist Church in Kansas City, Missouri. He is the award-winning author of more than ten books, including *Gospel Wakefulness*, *The Imperfect Disciple*, and *Unparalleled: How Christianity's Uniqueness Makes It Compelling*. Wilson's blog, *The Gospel-Driven Church*, is hosted by The Gospel Coalition, and he speaks at numerous churches and conferences around the world. He lives with his wife and two daughters outside Kansas City.

NOTES

Chapter 1: The Problem with Your Inner Life

1. You can watch Ray expound on the Immanuel Mantra at https://vimeo.com/59326626.

Chapter 2: The Promise of Mysterious Power

1. For a greater exploration of how the biblical miracles serve the overall mission of God, I have previously written *The Wonder-Working God: Seeing the Glory of Jesus in His Miracles* (Wheaton, IL: Crossway, 2014).
2. George Herbert, "The Holy Scriptures," in *The Temple* (London: Pickering, 1850), 51.
3. Sereno E. Dwight, "Memoirs of Jonathan Edwards," in *The Works of Jonathan Edwards*, ed. Edward Hickman (Edinburgh: Banner of Truth, 1974), 1:xiii.
4. Jonathan Edwards, "A Treatise Concerning Religious Affections," in *The Works of President Edwards* (New York: Leavitt and Allen, 1857), 3:69.
5. J. D. Greear, *Jesus Continued: Why the Spirit Inside You Is Better Than Jesus Beside You* (Grand Rapids: Zondervan, 2014), 64–65.

Chapter 3: Pressing "Reset" Every Day

1. Thomas N. Robinson et al., "Effects of Fast Food Branding on Young Children's Taste Preferences," *Archives of Pediatrics and*

Adolescent Medicine, 161, no. 8 (2007): 792–97, doi:10.1001/archpedi.161.8.792.

2. Robert D. Putnam, *Bowling Alone: The Collapse and Revival of American Community* (New York: Simon & Schuster, 2000).

3. Ibid., 19.

4. Quoted in Milton Meltzer, *Mark Twain Himself: A Pictorial Biography* (Columbia: University of Missouri Press, 2002), 82–83.

5. Henry David Thoreau, *Walden; or, Life in the Woods* (Boston: Houghton Mifflin, 1893), 15.

6. See, for instance, Frederick Dale Bruner and William Hordern, *The Holy Spirit: Shy Member of the Trinity* (Eugene, OR: Wipf and Stock, 2001).

7. C. S. Lewis, *Mere Christianity* (New York: Harper One, 1980), 26–27.

8. Robert Mark Kamen, *The Karate Kid*, directed by John G. Avildsen (Culver City, CA: Columbia Pictures, 1984), DVD.

9. Sinclair Ferguson, "The Reformed View," in *Christian Spirituality: Five Views of Sanctification*, ed. Donald Alexander (Downers Grove, IL: InterVarsity, 1988), 66.

Chapter 4: Engaging the Divine Dialogue

1. Shūsaku Endō, *Silence*, trans. William Johnston (New York: Taplinger, 1980), 97.

2. Ibid., 116–17.

3. Malcolm Moore, "Mother Teresa's '40-Year Faith Crisis,'" *Telegraph*, August 24, 2007, http://www.telegraph.co.uk/news/worldnews/1561247/Mother-Teresas-40-year-faith-crisis.html.

4. Francis A. Schaeffer, *He Is There and He Is Not Silent* (Carol Stream, IL: Tyndale, 1984), 87.

5. Ibid.

6. J. I. Packer, *Truth and Power: The Place of Scripture in the Christian Life* (Wheaton, IL: Shaw, 1996), 192–93.

7. Ibid., 209.

Chapter 5: The Spiritual Power of Prayer

1. Jared C. Wilson, *The Imperfect Disciple* (Grand Rapids: Baker, 2017).

2. John Piper, "Prayer and Predestination: A Dialogue Between Prayerful and Prayerless," Desiring God (blog), February 14, 1996, http://www.desiringgod.org/articles/prayer-and-predestination.

3. J. I. Packer, *Evangelism and the Sovereignty of God* (Downers Grove, IL: InterVarsity, 2012), 15.

4. Joe Thorn, *Experiencing the Trinity* (Wheaton, IL: Crossway, 2015), 53.

Chapter 6: The Blessing of Going Without

1. Eugene Peterson, *A Long Obedience in the Same Direction* (Downers Grove, IL: InterVarsity, 2000).

2. G. K. Chesterton, *A Miscellany of Men* (New York: Dodd, Mead, and Company, 1912), 303.

3. Laura Clark, "How Halitosis Became a Medical Condition with a 'Cure,'" Smithsonian.com, January 29, 2015, http://www .smithsonianmag.com/smart-news/marketing-campaign-invented -halitosis-180954082/.

4. Shaun Groves, "Home Wrecked," Shaun Groves (blog), February 27, 2008, http://shaungroves.com/2008/02/home-wrecked/.

Chapter 7: Breaking Free from the Drama

1. John Calvin, *Institutes of the Christian Religion*, trans. Ford Lewis Battles (Philadelphia: Westminster, 1960), I.xi.8, 108.

2. Trevin Wax, "Famous Quotes from Martin Luther," The Gospel Coalition, October 27, 2007, https://blogs.thegospelcoalition.org /trevinwax/2007/10/27/famous-quotes-from-martin-luther/.

3. Edward T. Welch, *When People Are Big and God Is Small* (Phillipsburg, NJ: P&R, 1997).

4. Jeff Vanderstelt, *Saturate: Being Disciples of Jesus in the Everyday Stuff of Life* (Wheaton, IL: Crossway, 2015), 175.

5. Larry Norman, "Readers Digest," on *Only Visiting This Planet*, Verve, 1972.

6. J. Ryan Lister, *The Presence of God* (Wheaton, IL: Crossway, 2015), 309.

Chapter 8: Holding On to Hope When the Days Are Dark

1. Raymond C. Ortlund Jr., *Supernatural Living for Natural People: The Life-Giving Message of Romans Eight* (Fearn, Scotland: Christian Focus, 2001), 109.
2. Wesley Hill, *Washed and Waiting: Reflections on Christian Faithfulness and Homosexuality* (Grand Rapids: Zondervan, 2010), 71.
3. Ibid., 71–72.
4. Michael Kelley, *Wednesdays Were Pretty Normal* (Nashville: B&H, 2012), 217–18.
5. Dietrich Bonhoeffer, *Life Together* (San Francisco: Harper and Row, 1954), 23.
6. Ross Douthat, *Bad Religion: How We Became a Nation of Heretics* (New York: Free Press, 2012), 205.
7. Ortlund, *Supernatural Living*, 107.

Chapter 9: Finding the Energy to Go the Distance

1. Dallas Willard, *Renovation of the Heart* (Colorado Springs: NavPress, 2002), 166.
2. Wayne Grudem, *Systematic Theology* (Grand Rapids: Zondervan, 1994), 1016.
3. Richard Lovelace provides some helpful insight on the historical trajectory of the "push and pull" over charismatic giftings, renewal movements, and spiritual "enthusiasm" in the church in his book *Dynamics of Spiritual Life* (Downers Grove, IL: InterVarsity, 1979).
4. Sam Storms, *Practicing the Power: Welcoming the Gifts of the Holy Spirit in Your Life* (Grand Rapids: Zondervan, 2017), 256.
5. Epiphanius, *The Panarion* 48:1.5, trans. Frank Williams (New York: E. J. Brill, 1994), 7.
6. Augustine, *The City of God*, trans. Marcus Dods (New York: Random House, 1950), xxii.8, 828.

7. D. A. Carson, *Showing the Spirit: A Theological Exposition of 1 Corinthians 12–14* (Grand Rapids: Baker, 1987), 166.
8. On this subject, I recommend most highly Carson, *Showing the Spirit*, and Storms, *Practicing the Power*.

Chapter 10: The Powerful Promises of God

1. Richard Lovelace, *Dynamics of Spiritual Life* (Downers Grove, IL: InterVarsity, 1979), 85.
2. Craig S. Keener, *Gift and Giver: The Holy Spirit for Today* (Grand Rapids: Baker, 2001), 169.